BEYOND
THE MONEY

**A Practical Guide for Successful Men
Leaving Full-time Work**

BY STEVE MENDL

Printed in Australia by McPherson's Printing Group
Text design by Charlotte Gelin Design
Cover design by Designerbility
Editing by Grammar Factory

 A catalogue record for this book is available from the National Library of Australia

Disclaimer
The material in this publication is of the nature of general comment only, and does not represent professional advice. It is not intended to provide specific guidance for particular circumstances and it should not be relied on as the basis for any decision to take action or not take action on any matter which it covers. Readers should obtain professional advice where appropriate, before making any such decision. To the maximum extent permitted by law, the author and publisher disclaim all responsibility and liability to any person, arising directly or indirectly from any person taking or not taking action based on the information in this publication.

Contents

Part 2: The 7 Wealth Areas Beyond Money

Introduction

Times are changing. So much so that coming generations may find this publication irrelevant. These days, Gen Y Millennials in the workforce have a different approach to their careers, experience of an increased rate of change, and diverse expectations when it comes to employment – and what comes after.

However, for three generations of men – Post-Depression, Baby Boomers and some Gen Xers – the move into the next stage of their life after full-time work is a big one, often filled with questions about identity, purpose and how to meaningfully fill the days of the next twenty-five years or so.

When successful men make the move out of full-time work into the next stage of their life, many are challenged by the transition. Though they've got the finances sorted, money's the first – and often only – thing they tend to concern themselves with beforehand, when it's actually the last thing they need to worry about. Beyond the money, there's now an extra forty to sixty hours a week that they have failed to plan and prepare for.

Money is important. It allows us, in modern western society, to live our desired lifestyle. However, it is not the only part of life that will provide happiness, joy and meaning when you move out of full-time employment and transition into the next stage of your life.

I have two dads – my biological father Peter and my stepfather John. Both are smart men who have achieved a lot in their lives so far. I have seen them go through very different journeys as they've left full-time employment and begun the rest of their lives, one alone and one together with my mother Kay.

My father Peter is a cautious man who very much cares about the impression he gives and his reputation. He has lived his years after leaving work very much the way he lived his work life. Prim, proper, tried and true, stiff upper lip and all that. Dad internalises everything and spends a lot of time planning... especially for the unexpected. He is what I call a 'JIC-er' – a Just In Caser. He plans and prepares for anything that can go wrong and all contingencies, most of which don't happen.

In contrast, my stepfather couldn't give a shit what other people think and sees life all up as a chance for never-ending adventures and challenges. His motto is: 'I'm going to wear out, not rust out.' My stepfather is an ideas man and doer in every sense of the word, often at the expense of planning a little further down life's track.

Both men's stories and journeys illustrate the highs and lows, the triumphs and challenges, and the contributions and legacies of men making the transition from full-time work into the next stage of their lives and beyond.

When it came to leaving full-time work, my father Peter did it in stages, transitioning from full-time work to part-time work and then focusing on charity and community work. The initial few months of the next stage of his life after he had established his own version of financial security were enjoyable and included regular games of golf, community service meetings, and work alumni gatherings. Life was good.

However, within a year, my father was diagnosed with renal issues (kidney disease) and within two years he was on home dialysis. This had a huge effect on his energy, his time (between six and eight hours of dialysis several nights a week) and his ability to fully enjoy the next stage of his life. My father's tale is not a rare one. Many of my clients and other people I know have shared stories of men who stopped work and within a few years developed diseases for no apparent reason.

Despite my father's illness, he focused his energy on making a difference in the community and through his work with the Lions Club, which he had been a member of for over thirty years and where he went on to hold the position of District Governor. This was his new purpose and he performed his role well up until his death.

His focus on community did have a price, however. My father lost a key romantic relationship due to his new vision. In later years, he shared with me that it was one of his greatest regrets. He also shared that his new purpose and status in the next stage of his life within a large organisation masked a private matter. My father suffered from a very private depression. Public joy, private hell, I would call it. Coming from a British/Australian upbringing, like his father before him, the old soldier's cry of 'maintaining a stiff upper lip' rang true for my father. So, talking to someone about his feelings and what he was going through was not an option he considered. From his point of view, it would have been seen as weakness.

My stepfather John has a very different story but with some similar strains. After many years with the government, he retired with a pension. When he met my mother, he was already well on his way to transitioning into the next stage of his life.

After work, my stepfather turned his passions, interests and hobbies into activities that made for a busy life. He returned to his first role as an apprentice mechanic and restored cars over many years. One of them was a 1954 Bentley that he restored over more than ten years. He turned an interest in gaming into a consultancy and embarked on various entrepreneurial ventures. Even over eighty, he still has ideas that he turns into business opportunities and, with my mother, travels the country and the world wheeling, dealing and trading.

An avid reader, my stepfather keeps his mind active by reading a combination of fiction and non-fiction. One activity that he has continued for many years is his interest in collectables. Watches, coins, pens, stamps – you name it – he likes the thrill of trading... buying low and selling for a profit.

Both fathers exercised after coming out of full-time work. My father walked and used the gym provided in the village complex. My stepfather ran (including undertaking the City to Surf at eighty-three), walked and has been the oldest attendee at the Australian Institute of Sport for years.

Although both fathers continued to be active, both have had times when they have had to ride the roller-coaster that is life. During the transition, both went through some fear, some frustration, some confusion, some stress... it is the nature of change.

Probably the greatest legacy that both of my fathers have left is their overall perspective on life in general. For my father, it was: 'Always look on the bright side,' for my stepfather: 'I'm going to wear out... not rust out.' Both have shown a great love for life in all its forms and refused to submit to the myths around men moving into the next stage of their lives.

Part of the challenge we face is around busting the myths ingrained in our society.

BUSTING THE MYTHS AND FACING THE REALITIES

There are plenty of myths and different opinions out there about leaving full-time work. Most are based on the experiences of a generation or two ago, when life expectancies were shorter, people were less healthy in later life, and there were fewer lifestyle options.

It's important to understand that many of these myths arbitrarily limit the options available to you as you move out of full-time employment. They restrict you, because you've consciously or unconsciously ruled things out before even considering them.

Here's a quick Myth Versus Reality quiz to test the accuracy of your expectations.

Answer 'Yes' or 'No' to each of the following statements:

- Most successful men transitioning out of full-time work are totally satisfied doing nothing but travelling and relaxing in the next stage of their lives.

- Many men report that the single greatest problem in the early days is restructuring their daily lives.

- Preparing a résumé is nothing but a waste of time for successful men who don't plan to work for pay.

- Significant others have little trouble adjusting to their partner being at home most of the time.

- If someone has a consuming interest, like golf, they are always happy to spend all their spare time pursuing it – they do not need to plan other activities.

- Because many friendships revolve around the workplace, many successful men find that they have to consciously and actively work at expanding their social networks.

- At age sixty-five, you can expect to live at least another fifteen years.

- When modifying one's diet, it is easiest to eliminate all undesirable foods and add only desirable ones in one clean sweep.

- The majority of successful men report that they are very pleased with their new lives after leaving work.

Perhaps you're on the mark… but perhaps not. Throughout the book, you'll gain a realistic perspective from which to look at your options (but if you want to cheat and find out right away, the answers are in an appendix at the back of the book!).

Before we move on, perhaps you're wondering how I have the answers, so here's a little about me.

MY STORY

I began my working life at eleven years old, in a kitchen. I helped prepare food with my mother, who ran an executive catering business.

Throughout my childhood, the work I really dreamed of doing was playing cricket for Australia. However, when I was twelve, I was diagnosed with acute lymphoblastic leukaemia and my perspective shifted dramatically. In the wards of the Prince of Wales Hospital in Sydney, 300 kilometres from my home town of Canberra, I learnt very quickly that there are a lot more important things in life than sport. I also learnt early that there is a lot more to life than money.

While recovering from leukaemia, I was introduced to Camp Quality, a camp for young children living with cancer, and CanTeen, an organisation for teenagers living with cancer. Between the ages of fifteen and twenty-five, I devoted my time to study and the education of the public on the teenage journey through the treatment and survival of cancer. I did this mainly through my work with CanTeen, as co-founder of the ACT Division, and later as National President and Chair of the Board.

It was my passion for helping people that led me to a career as an educator, business coach and executive mentor, quick to recognise that leaving full-time employment is one of the greatest career transitions of all.

My mission over the next ten to fifteen years is to educate, assist and empower as many men as possible to make the most of their lives after leaving full-time work. My passion for this mission has come not only from seeing my fathers go through the changes involved, both good and bad, but from having assisted thousands of people making transitions in their lives over the past twenty years.

THE PROBLEM WITH 'RETIREMENT'

The *Oxford English Dictionary* definition of retirement is: *The action or fact of leaving one's job and ceasing to work.* The emphasis is on ceasing work in all its forms. That's why you won't find me using the word retirement much at all in this book after this introduction – as I don't see myself as working with retired people. In the 21st century, with anywhere between another twenty to forty years to live and given both a functioning brain and reasonably able body, I just don't see leaving full-time employment as entering 'retirement'.

I see it as entering what some have referred to as your Second Adulthood or your Third Age. I choose to refer to it as the next age or next stage of your life. And I use the word stage deliberately. We all play different roles throughout our lives. Part of the aim of this book is to inspire you to consider what roles you would like to play in the coming years. The options are many and may be short, medium or long term in nature. The choice is yours.

Today's workforce leavers are exiting employment earlier and remaining healthy for longer. Many people will be retired for almost as many years as they have worked and their lifestyles will reflect a level of activity beyond yesterday's stereotype.

Today's active 'Next-Ager' has many options:

- Learn something new, perhaps even return to school.
- Start a small business or begin consulting in an area of expertise.
- Undertake an ambitious physical fitness program.
- Work part time in a chosen industry.
- Develop an investment portfolio and play an active role in its development.
- Focus on more traditional areas of leisure – travel, sport and family.

Society is increasingly accepting and supportive of people who select these expanded options. But this increased variety of choice presents challenges as well as opportunities. The initial challenge is to select activities and goals that are right for you. The next challenge is to formulate and carry out an action plan incorporating the ideal mix of activities to meet the goals you've set for yourself.

What roles will you play in the years ahead? Some of you may do part-time, casual or volunteer work, some of you may become consultants in your chosen areas of expertise, and some of you may choose not to do any conventional work but embrace a different lifestyle, taking up new hobbies and interests, perhaps even in a different location. You will have the opportunity to work on yourself, your health, your relationships and even your spiritual development. There are no right or wrong answers. You just need to recognise that there is a world of wealth out there to enjoy.

THE 7 WEALTH AREAS

Having seen the transition out of full-time work done well and not so well, I have found that most men have a clear idea of where they are situated financially, but planning for other areas of life is lacking, has been avoided or is non-existent.

Many have an idea that they will do up the house or go and see the world, but once the home looks great or the travel is done, there are often still decades of life left to engage with – and not being prepared for them is stressful, even with the savings there to cover the costs of day-to-day living and a prosperous lifestyle.

This book is presented in three parts:

PART 1: BE PREPARED – The first part of the book is all about preparation and why preparation is key when it comes to taking control of your life and managing the transition well.

PART 2: THE 7 WEALTH AREAS – The second part of the book will take you step by step through the seven wealth areas to consider beyond money, so you can plan what areas you wish to nurture in the next stage of your life, with awareness of the inherent challenges and opportunities.

1. **YOUR SELF:**

   This section is about taking time to join the two out of ten people who really make the effort to reflect on what is important to them. This is where you can create supporting beliefs that assist you on your journey into the next age. In this section, you get clear on: your values; your beliefs (current and future); and your motivated skills. By clearly identifying what is important to you, what skills motivate you, and what you want to learn, use or share, you create a practical blueprint for the next stage of your life.

2. **YOUR WELLBEING:**

   Health is Wealth, even more so as you move into the next stage of your life. This section provides frameworks and some easy-to-apply guidance for you to follow when it comes to your wellbeing, covering: food and nutrition, physical fitness and mental health. In this section, you will be introduced to the 7 Ancient Principles of Wellbeing.

3.   YOUR LOCATION:

Location, location, location, as they say in the real estate game. It's an important consideration in the next stage of your life. Where are you going to live? For what reasons? Have you done your due diligence? All of these questions are explored in this section and more, with options presented to make this wealth area come to life for you and help you avoid 'Rose-coloured Glasses Syndrome'.

4.   YOUR RELATIONSHIPS:

Arguably one of the most important wealth areas beyond money, this section explores your relationships and the idea of open communication as you move into the next stage of your life. What are your expectations of family members, friends and social networks? The wealth inherent in your relationships is the real key to long-term enjoyment of the next stage of your life.

5.   YOUR LIFESTYLE:

This section investigates the question: What lifestyle do you want to create? It covers both recreational activities and the concept of a modified work life. Considering hobbies, interests, continuing self-development, amusements, sports and volunteer work, a series of frameworks are provided in order to unpack your head and get your ideas onto paper.

6. **YOUR LEGACY:**

    What is the legacy that you wish to leave? What
    contribution do you wish to make? This section
    emphasises that there is no right or wrong when it
    comes to what you want to leave behind when you are
    not on the planet any more. This wealth area is about
    making your own contribution in your own way – a way
    that makes a difference.

7. **YOUR SPIRITUAL DEVELOPMENT:**

    With an open mind and broad definitions, this section
    shares two concepts that many men have found useful
    in the next stage of their lives: the Law of Attraction and
    the simple practice of gratitude. The section provides
    some practical strategies for engaging with both,
    encouraging you to explore your perspective on the
    world around you and see how that shapes what you
    focus on and what you can achieve.

PART 3: FORM A PLAN – The third part of the book is about
making a plan. This is how strategy becomes action and
action becomes reality.

Throughout the book, you will find simple and practical
exercises and tips that will assist you to move proactively
into the next stage of your life.

As an old man once said, 'Life is a journey, not a destination.'
There's no better time than now to prepare for your next
journey. The journey to becoming a Next-Ager. So let's go!

Part One:
Be Prepared

'Become a student of change.
It is the only thing that will remain constant.'

– ANTHONY D'ANGELO

Part One
Be Prepared

1. Welcoming Change

The secret of change is to focus all of your energy,
not on fighting the old, but on building the new.

— SOCRATES

(Dan Millman, *Way of the Peaceful Warrior*)

One day, a man in his late fifties entered my office. He was shaking. By the look on his face, I could tell how scared he was. As we spoke, it became clear that he was in shock. After thirty-plus years working for the same company, he'd received the news that his role had been made redundant. His original vision of being with the company he had been so loyal to for his whole working life was gone.

As we got to know each other, he shared that his biggest fear was that no one would want him at his age. Although he was financially secure, he couldn't imagine a day without work.

Although Jeff's transition was a forced one, and the decision made was outside of his control, this is the same thing I see with clients who are about to transition out of full-time employment simply because the time has come. They just can't imagine it. They aren't prepared for it – even though they know it's coming.

I asked Jeff whether he had prepared for such an eventuality as redundancy, given the onward decline of the business over the past few years and the redundancies that had already hit the company. His view had been that he was too valuable to the company and the team that he led to have to consider it.

He didn't see it coming, despite the signs. In contrast, leaving work because that time has arrived is something that people can see coming. But, equally, they don't prepare.

I asked what Jeff had enjoyed about the role he had been doing. His answer was the team. I asked about the role itself and it turned out he hadn't enjoyed much of the last fifteen years in management at all, even though the money was good. It's a story I've heard often in my work. But even though he hadn't been fulfilled in his role, he was stressed and scared about the change to come. Despite being financially secure, he was at a loss when it came to the future.

I asked him about what he might want to do next. His answer was, 'I don't know.' I rephrased the question and asked what he might enjoy doing in a work situation. But he replied again, 'I don't know.'

Like so many professional men that I've worked with, Jeff had been so involved in doing his job and looking after his team that he had not prepared in any way, except financially, for what might be in store around the corner. Even with awareness of the changes happening around him and within the company he worked for, he'd turned a blind eye. He hadn't prepared himself for any change.

When it comes to career transitions – and especially the greatest career transition of all when you leave the work-force altogether – preparation is a key factor in making the journey into your next life stage smooth and stress-free.

The solution comes in two parts. The first part is obvious: plan for the change early. There is evidence to suggest that change within companies is happening at a quicker rate than ever before. This is due to several factors. Firstly, advancing technology is shaping and re-shaping industries at an ever increasing rate. Secondly, in many industries, CEOs and other senior managers are not staying as long as they have done in previous generations. Each time there is a change in CEO, there is inevitably 'restructuring', 'future proofing' or 'workforce transformation' that results in disruption to the status quo. Further, mergers and acquisitions are happening many times quicker than they used to. The result is often the need to deal with duplication of roles, cost efficiencies and new directions. Many people find themselves losing their old roles. Companies are looking to becoming lighter and more agile in an increasingly competitive and technological marketplace, so, in today's climate, planning early is essential for dealing efficiently with any change.

The second part of the solution is around changing your perspective. You need to cultivate a perspective of expecting change. The Generation Y Millennials are extremely good at adapting to change. This is because it has been a constant part of their lives, both in terms of technology and in terms of moving freely within the workforce. This is something that older generations need to adapt to, and learn to expect.

Planning early and shifting your perspective to expect constant change rather than things remaining constant are key to combatting the natural fear of change that comes with not knowing – or being able to imagine – what the future might hold.

In short, we need to welcome change. If there is one thing certain in life, things change. Being open to this and accepting it as part of life when it arrives means it becomes easier to deal with.

Many people believe that Charles Darwin coined the phrase 'survival of the fittest'. And most believe it means the strongest, smartest and fastest animals will survive. In fact, Darwin actually taught us that the most 'flexible' life forms within a certain system are the ones that will survive and thrive. It is called the Law of Requisite Variety.

Some sixty-five million years ago, dinosaurs were the kings of the earth. They were some of the biggest, fastest and smartest animals on the planet. We've come to believe in the early stages of the 21st century that an unexpected mass extinction level event occurred. It was an asteroid that collided with the earth in the Gulf of Mexico and, within a relatively short period of time, the dinosaurs were wiped out. The reason was that they were not flexible and agile enough to survive the severe and dramatic climate change (a very long, toxic winter) and the ice age that followed. So, what animals did survive and thrive? The humble cockroach did, by having a strong radiation tolerance and constitution. Crocodiles and alligators did, by being able to spend time in the water as semi-aquatic animals. And sharks, turtles, frogs and various species of birds all survived, thrived and evolved into what we see today.

The next-ager who is strong, smart and fast but not agile and flexible as they move into the next stage of their life will be like the dinosaur. They won't die, but the transition will be harder than it needs to be, with fear, frustration, confusion and stress ruling their lives until they either get sick with a disease or get assistance and move through the struggle into acceptance and creativity.

Those next-agers who are flexible and adaptable to change are more likely to be in a position to make the most of the transition and thrive in the next stage of their lives.

Welcome the change. It is inevitable, so plan for it, not only now but also into the future.

In Jeff's case, initial planning would have allowed him to be more aware of what was happening within his industry and within his own company. This would have opened him up to anticipating the end result and he could have worked to become flexible enough to be ready to move on and into the next stage of his life without the shock and anxiety that he experienced.

'Most businesses don't plan to fail; they fail to plan,' my business management teacher used to say. So it is with moving from full-time work into the next stage of your life.

In an ideal world, the preparation for leaving your last full-time role should come well before you actually leave.

Planning is easy when you know what you're planning for.

But what exactly *are* you planning for? What are you going to have to deal with? The next chapter will consider the tricky nature of the changes you're up against.

2. A Change of Identity

*'The value of identity of course
is that so often with it comes purpose.'*

— RICHARD GRANT

Since the introduction of superannuation, money has been the main focus when it comes to leaving full-time employment, often to the exclusion of all else.

However, this overlooks the fact that there are many different facets when it comes to preparation. The challenges are numerous – mentally and physically, psychologically and energetically. These areas are rarely focused on.

A survey conducted out of the USA through the Trans America Center of Retirement Studies revealed that forty-one per cent of respondents reported moving out of full-time work as being more stressful than either the transition into marriage or changing previous jobs. Most of them indicated that they had not been prepared enough for the reality of having another thirty-five to sixty hours a week on their hands. A more recent survey of 1,000 new retirees (within five years of retirement) conducted by the Centre for Ageing Better in the UK discovered that twenty per cent of people found the transition difficult. This is particularly the case for men.

Part of this is due to a crisis of identity. For 60,000+ years, the primary role of men has been to provide for the family and/or the extended social community. As society has developed, we have moved away from hunting and gathering to earning Money (more accurately currency in the 21st century) with which to buy the essentials – and the not so essentials – for our lives. As men, this drive to provide is in our DNA and pre-programmed into our biology, most notably through our limbic flight or fight responses.

In his book *David and Goliath*, Malcom Gladwell looks closely at Samuel Stouffer's concept of relative deprivation and how it plays out in various environments.

Relative deprivation is the idea that by comparing and evaluating yourself against a cohort or people you spend a lot of time with, there is the perception that you are not doing as well as others. Relative deprivation is also called the 'Big Fish Little Pond Effect'.

In the study explored in the book, Stoufler found that there were similar statistics across many universities, regardless of whether they were up-market and prestigious, like Harvard, Yale or the University of California, or perceived to be poorer or less selective public institutions.

In a nutshell, it is not how smart you are, it is how smart you feel relative to other people in your various environments that drives your self-perception and your identity. Really, it's how you feel that matters.

In a university situation, the smarter you think your peers are, the dumber you feel. The dumber you feel, the more likely you are to drop out of university.

So how does this idea of relative deprivation relate to the journey out of full-time work? When leaving employment, relative deprivation can combine with relevance deprivation.

When leaving employment, relative deprivation may arise in the perception that another man who has just entered the next stage of their life may be doing better than you, that they have 'their shit in order' so to speak: they have a better car, they have just been on a luxury cruise to Alaska, etc. The danger here is that relative deprivation (comparing your internal experience with others in a similar situation) combined with the concept of relevance deprivation (the fact that the phone has stopped ringing and there are not as many invitations to corporate and other business functions) has a big effect on your confidence and sense of identity.

Leaving full-time work, many men lose a sense of their identity altogether. They've been able to answer the question 'What do you do?' with certainty for so many years and have normally associated themselves with a certain role. The question becomes harder when you're no longer working. You suddenly have to think about what you are going to say.

Through my work, I have observed so many men who have their identity wrapped up in their job or job title, whether it be CEO, COO, CFO, lawyer, senior manager, supervisor, farmer, etc. I have dealt with men who find it hard to let go of the labels. So much so that they'll usually stick to them in some form; for example, by introducing themselves as the former CEO of ABC company.

For many successful men, there is an addictive quality to having relevance within a group or company. This is inherent to many of the patriarchal aspects of the western society that we find ourselves in today.

This institutionalisation starts with schooling and continues right through our lives. Our ego needs to be fed and one of the ways to do this is through the creation of imaginary and illusionary temples and templates that support industry and commerce. However, there is a price to pay. That comes in the emotional withdrawal that occurs once the status is removed in the movement out of full-time work and into the next stage of your life.

In a business setting and hierarchy, it is easy to measure your success and relevance. Indeed, by the very nature of modern western society, there is status that comes with promotions and entering higher roles. This is particularly so for successful men.

When leaving full-time work, the status and relevance goes… and with that can come feelings of loss and uncertainty. This is why the mental preparation for the shift out of full-time work needs to come well before the shift itself.

It is time to be your own man, to be yourself, not a label you've worn in a business – never mind how many years you've worn it. Be free.

For many, this process is mentally painful. Without awareness and support, it can lead to substance abuse and/ or depression. For others, this process can be extremely liberating. The aim of this book is to make it the latter.

However, becoming free of the work labels isn't the end of the story. It's not just out in the world but at home that things change. You're not just shaking off an old identity; you're forging a new one.

Let's take an everyday but very true-to-life example.

Joe was embarking on the first day of the rest of his life. He had slept in (until 7.00 am), he had had a leisurely breakfast with his wife at their home, and he had read the papers from front to back for the first time in many years.

He sat in his dedicated chair in the lounge room and was contemplating what to do for the remainder of the day, a tricky question since he hadn't had this much time on his hands before – ever. As he sat there, he heard the postie coming by and stopping at the house. So Joe thought it would be a great idea to collect whatever the postie had dropped in the post box.

As he was heading out the door, his wife followed him out and into the front garden. She asked him what he was doing. Joe replied, bemused, 'I'm collecting the post!' But Joe's wife responded, 'Oh no, you're not. That has been my job for the last thirty-five years and that is not going to change today or any day soon.'

So there Joe was, on the first day of the rest of his life, trying to be useful and instead having an argument on the front lawn with his wife about who would collect the letters in the post box.

It may be a small matter and seem insignificant, but this shift from full-time employment to the next stage of your life involves many people around you. Just like you, each one of them has routines, rituals and habits that they have formed in accordance with the particular roles they play. You must be aware of these and consider how they will change as you spend more time at home than ever before.

The key here is to not assume anything either before or after the transition, especially with the loved ones who are close to you and whom you have spent a lot of time with in the past. The old saying is very pertinent here: don't assume anything – when you assume, it makes an ass out of you and me.

As you can see, this sense of shifting identity can be a minefield. How do you navigate it? Again, it comes down to preparation. In the next chapter, we're going to look at the journey through a transition in terms of different phases you travel through. The second part of the book will address the wealth areas you can plan to make the most of, including devoting time to working on your sense of self and identity, and nurturing your relationships with others in the next stage of your life.

3. Changing Trains

'Change is never a loss, it is only change.'

— VERNON HOWARD

Recent studies from the US uncovered several interesting findings. Among them was the fact that nearly two thirds (sixty-three per cent) of recently retired Baby Boomers said they felt stressed about retirement leading up to the decision. But only one in four said they remained stressed after having been retired for some time.

These studies were performed by the Ameriprise Financial, who released the results after surveying a thousand newly retired adults between the ages of sixty and sixty-three, and the TransAmerica Center for Retirement Studies.

Despite the emotional challenges of the transition into retirement, sixty-five per cent of the participants surveyed fell into a new routine fairly quickly. Half said they expected to have more free time once they retired. Forty-three per cent said they were having more fun in retirement, and the majority – fifty-seven per cent – reported they were very satisfied with their situation.

About one in ten respondents said they returned to work in some capacity, but most of those working for pay said that they were not really working for the money but rather because the job seemed like an interesting opportunity. They wanted intellectual stimulation and social interaction.

It makes me wonder what they were doing beforehand. In my opinion, you've got to enjoy the work that you do, and it's a shame to come across so many people in the course of *my* work who have been very attached to their job all their life, but have not actually enjoyed it.

The most important aspects of this particular survey were the findings that:

- Nearly one in three respondents said the hardest thing about retiring was making emotional adjustments, such as losing connections with colleagues;

- Thirty-two per cent said their greatest difficulty was getting used to a different routine; and

- Twenty-two per cent reported that one of the hardest things to do was find purpose and ways to pass the time.

These issues are where planning and preparation are really key in coping with the transition.

One of my clients, Roger, once shared a metaphor regarding how he was able to deal with leaving full-time work. He saw the transition into the next stage of his life as being like changing trains at a station. In his work life, he had always caught the express train to and from home. In the next stage of his life, he decided to catch a more relaxed and slower train.

One of the weeks leading up to his movement out of full-time employment, he deliberately took longer to get to work and return home in the evening. He got to work a bit late and he left a little early. He had longer lunches. He was changing to a slower train.

He was still active, still moving; however, this time it was going to be at his own pace, off the express train he'd taken for so many years.

Roger's approach is a great way to embrace change and mentally prepare for the next stage in life.

At this point, I'd like to introduce you to the William Bridges Model of Change, developed by change consultant William Bridges. As you transition out of full-time employment, it is worth considering the different phases in the process in relation to this model.

It is important to acknowledge that although the model is presented as a flowing and linear process, it is really an isolating process where you can think you are in creativity and acceptance one day and then wake the next day and be in fear or confusion.

Each person reacts differently to change. The reason that I present this model is to share with you what most people go through unconsciously. In doing so, you can consider how to deal with things appropriately when the feelings and reactions arise for you.

With awareness, you can monitor where you are operating from on a day-to-day basis. You can accept where you are and look for a way in which to move yourself through the curve into a more resourceful or useful state.

The three phases, or stages, you find in a major change or transition are detailed below:

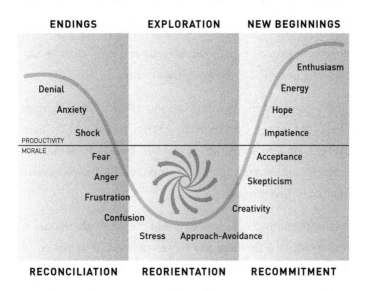

| ENDINGS | EXPLORATION | NEW BEGINNINGS |

Denial
Anxiety
Shock

PRODUCTIVITY

MORALE

Fear
Anger
Frustration
Confusion
Stress   Approach-Avoidance

Enthusiasm
Energy
Hope
Impatience
Acceptance
Skepticism
Creativity

| RECONCILIATION | REORIENTATION | RECOMMITMENT |

PHASE 1: WHEN WORK LIFE ENDS
– ENDINGS/RECONCILIATION

If you have the choice to make the transition on your own terms, then you may only experience one of the first three emotions that you find listed in the first curve of the first stage. If your role has been made redundant, or you have to cease work far earlier than expected, then you may experience two or all three.

When a period of life or a cherished relationship comes to an end, most people have a difficult time letting go of it. During this time of learning, called the 'Ending' by Bridges, one can feel sadness mixed with anger over the loss.

Further, as we've discussed, as a man transitioning out of full-time work, you will likely be giving up your identity; for example, as a man in the corporate world.

You had a routine, a place to go every day where people knew and respected you, where you received daily acknowledgement for your work accomplishments. You had a well-defined role, a comfort zone in which to operate.

For many high-achieving men, it is understandably difficult to let the past go and move forward.

The process of Ending, or 're-solution' as I like to call it, can, for some, take a matter of weeks. For others, it might be months. For still others, it can take longer, as they find themselves caught up in the emotions of anxiety, fear, frustration, confusion and stress. In some cases, this can lead to depression.

Leaving full-time work after a long time with a company means saying goodbye to the automatic greeting, 'I'm an ABC and I work with ABC Company.' For some, this can, in itself, reduce their self-esteem and damage their image.

Holding on is a normal and predictable reaction to major change. The most important thing to do is act in order to move on. Acknowledge and accept the feelings of change while leaning into the uncomfortable aspect of it all and progressing into the next stage.

If you are a man who has been heavily committed to providing for your family through work, then often this transition can be difficult and challenging. When one's energy has been so focused for so long, letting go of being a significant corporate employee and moving into a new stage of life and a new identity can be an unsettling journey.

Acknowledging this can be a strong first step.

I was watching an interview conducted with a highly regarded medical professional who was the CEO of a major hospital. The interview focused on the first few months of his move into the next stage of his life. When asked to tell his story, he shared that he had thought that he was ready and prepared for the next stage in his life. His last day at work included a twelve-hour day (very normal for him over the course of the last twenty-five years) and then a farewell function.

The next day, he was 'retired'. He shared that he had gone from a highly pressured work situation to absolutely nothing. After the first week, he was feeling 'edgy'. This turned very quickly into anxiety, even though he had no pressure on him at all. Eventually, he sought professional assistance. He fell off the 'retirement cliff' (something *Forbes* magazine describes in terms of cash flow – here it is all about the leap from full-time work to no work at all, it is the physical, mental and emotional 'cliff')

With too much time on his hands, his anxiety grew until it became detrimental to his ongoing health and his relationship with his wife.

This physical, mental and emotional response has nothing to do with logic. It is just a response to transitioning suddenly. When doing so, the mind and body don't have a chance to get used to the massive change. The medical professional shared that he regretted not spending more time mentally preparing and considering all the aspects outside of the money when it came to the idea of having sixty hours a week suddenly free. He said that if he did it again, he would do it in stages, leading himself gently into not working at all.

The story has a happy ending. After going through the fear, frustration, confusion and stress, then finally seeking assistance (which he encouraged anyone who needs help to do), the man got comfortable with his new identity and found new purpose on the boards of several not-for-profit organisations. He also went back to sailing, a sport he had done as a kid.

PHASE 2: WANDERING MIDDLE EARTH – EXPLORATION/REORIENTATION

During Bridges' Exploration phase, the man having left full-time work has accepted the reality of change and the loss of his old identity and activities, but has yet to develop something to take their place. This time is characterised by a feeling of being in limbo.

Here, you can feel somewhat lost. You are restless, questioning life's purpose, and making the effort to restructure time around meaningful goals. This phase, while often uncomfortable, rarely lasts too long (three to six months for most). And this can be after taking a break from it all (international trips are a favourite here).

A couple came to see me once. They sat down and simply said, 'We've been putting this off for too long, and now the critical mass of anxiety has hit us it is time to do something about it. But before we do, we are going on a break.' It wasn't until their return from a six-month, worldwide tour that we began working together. Sometimes, you have to give yourself a break.

What became clear as I worked with them was that going on a break actually became a metaphor for exploring and reorienting themselves, both individually and as a couple.

The break allowed them to return home with a clean slate, ready to create the next stage of their lives.

In Exploration, a successful man needs the support of others, as well as time alone to assess the new situation; it is common to feel sadness or confusion. The Reorientation phase is not a time of high energy or creativity; while you are still forming a new identity, it is not wise to act impulsively.

PHASE 3: WELCOME TO THE NEXT AGE – NEW BEGINNINGS/RECOMMITMENT

This phase is reached when you embrace your new role, having transitioned out of full-time employment. You feel ready to make a New Beginning, ready and able to plan the next stage in your life.

This stage is characterised by the sense of having an increasingly clear direction and the energy and confidence to carry out a new life plan. New goals are defined, as well as the strategies for achieving them. As new activities and relationships emerge, backward glances occur less frequently.

Those who have prepared over many years for the next stage of their life slowly begin to transfer their interests and non-working time over to hobbies, sports, socialising and other activities. This makes the transition all the easier. I have had a number of clients who have come though my door and, over the course of a few sessions, very clearly laid out the plans for activities and goals that they have developed over the previous few years.

They smoothly transition into being next-agers.

A conscious understanding of the transition process and the time it takes will help you transition from full-time employee to next-ager, better adjusting to this major change. It's the aim of the next part of the book to explore what goals and activities will provide you with the most wealth in the new world you're entering.

It's this kind of preparation and planning that will help you face the Ending, let go of your old identity and thrive in the times to come.

I ran into one of my more colourful clients on the golf course recently, having completed a program with them some time ago. It was a short conversation and he was happy with his new life. As we parted, he said, 'You know, that bastard Bridges was right; I've got more energy than I had six months ago. I love getting out onto the golf course when I can. I've dropped two shots on my handicap and plan to lose another two in the next year.'

'My wife loves that I get out of the house,' he added. 'A few months ago, I was just pissing her off by hanging around.'

Part 2:
The 7 Wealth Areas
Beyond Money

'Riches cannot always be measured in money.'

— NAPOLEON HILL

1. Self

'Man struggles to find life outside himself,
unaware that the life that he is seeking is within him.'

— KHALIL GIBRAN

Questions to consider in this part of the book:
- **Who are you?**
- **What's important to you?**
- **What do you believe?**

In philosophy, there are four great questions for humans to contemplate in the course of their lives:

- Who am I?
- Where did I come from?
- Why am I here?
- Where am I going?

A lot of men consider these questions on automatic pilot. From the time we are young children until we become old men, we are forever searching for ourselves, but often living someone else's version of ourselves.

I cannot promise you the answers to these questions in this section; however, I do encourage you to be Self-ish – explore what *you* value and what *you* believe at this point in time.

Our values and beliefs play an integral role in who we are as human beings. Together they are like an internal compass that evolves as we go through life, whether we are consciously aware of them or not. Some values and beliefs are useful, some not so useful, and others can leave us in a double bind that is hard to break.

The purpose of the following pages is to provide you with the kind of knowledge few people have of themselves. More to the point, it is about getting clear on what is important to you and what you believe, in alignment with your personal life values. By doing so, you get comfortable in your own skin as you move into the next stage of your life. You set the foundations for designing what you want moving forward and you give yourself the opportunity to leave your work identity behind.

YOUR VALUES

Essentially, your values are what are important to you. While many people think they know what's important to them, they don't often stop, sit down and truly think about what their core values are. We are going to get clear on your values so that you become more aware of them. This will allow you to see how they show up in your life on a day-to-day basis, how you can prioritise them, and how you can take them into consideration when planning the next stage in your life.

The most important thing to realise when you're dealing with values is that they belong to you, not to anyone else.

Though your values may have been influenced by your upbringing and your life experiences, they do not belong to your mother, your father, your grandparents, your siblings or any other people who might have played a significant role in your life. Your values must belong to you! So in this space, I encourage you to be quite 'selfish' – look at your life through your own eyes, not anyone else's.

My research over the past twenty years indicates that you could have anywhere up to 420 different defined values, which cover everything in life from your attitude to money right through to the way you approach your career. Below, I present an abbreviated list. Here's your chance to identify your life values right now, as you plan to move out of full-time employment and into the next stage of your life.

Exercise: Defining Your Values

Label each value from the list below with one of the following:

- **CV** for Core Value (always value)
- **OV** for Often Value
- **SV** for Sometimes Value
- **NV** for Never Value

By doing this, you begin to get a clear idea of what you always value, often value, sometimes value and never value. It is from your shortlist of CVs and OVs that you can go on to select your top ten values.

You may find you resonate with one of the values listed but don't entirely agree with its definition. In that case, add your own definition – this is all about what your values mean to you.

LIFE VALUES:

- **Abundance**: Plentifulness when it comes to the good things in life; prosperity in love, money, etc.

- **Achievement**: Successfully completing something with effort, skill or courage. Achieving outcomes.

- **Acknowledgement**: Receiving expressions of recognition, appreciation and gratitude for something.

- **Adventure**: Wanting unusual and exciting experiences or engaging in risky activities.

- **Advancement**: To develop and improve, seeking promotion in rank or status.

- **Affection**: A desire for feelings of fondness or liking by others.

- **Affluence**: A state of having a great deal of money or wealth.

- **Ambition**: Strong desire to do or achieve things.

- **Artistry**: To use a creative skill or ability.

- **Assertiveness**: Having or showing a confident and forceful personality.

- **Awareness**: Knowledge and/or perception of situations and facts.

- **Balance**: Situations in which different elements are equal or in correct proportions.

- **Beauty**: A combination of qualities that pleases someone.
- **Bliss**: State of perfect happiness or great joy; oblivious of everything else.
- **Bravery**: Courageous behaviour or character.
- **Brilliance**: Exceptional talent or intelligence.
- **Calmness**: The state of being free of agitation or strong emotion.
- **Celebrity**: State of being well known.
- **Certainty**: Knowing that something is the case. An air of confidence. The quality of being reliably true.
- **Challenge**: Tasks or situations that test your abilities.
- **Change**: Frequent alteration in content and setting.
- **Charity**: The voluntary giving of assistance either in time and/or money.
- **Cheerfulness**: State of being noticeably happy and optimistic.
- **Clarity**: Being clear and coherent about activities now and in the future.
- **Community**: People living in the same place or having characteristics in common.
- **Compassion**: Concern for other human beings.
- **Confidence**: The state of feeling certain about the truth of something and/or self-assurance arising from an appreciation of one's own abilities or qualities.
- **Connection**: A relationship with oneself or others. Association or linking one thing with another.

- **Contentment**: A state of happiness and satisfaction.

- **Conservation**: Preservation, protection or restoration of something in particular.

- **Contribution**: Playing a part in bringing about a result or assisting something or people to advance.

- **Control**: The power to influence or direct the course of events or people's behaviour.

- **Coolness**: The quality of being fashionably attractive or impressive. Freedom from excitement, anxiety or excessive emotion.

- **Courage**: Strength to do something that frightens one or demonstrating strength in the face of pain or grief.

- **Creativity**: The use of imagination or original ideas to create things: inventiveness.

- **Curiosity**: A strong desire to learn and discover new things.

- **Daring**: Adventurous or audaciously bold.

- **Delight**: To take great pleasure in. Please greatly.

- **Desire**: A strong feeling of wanting to have or do something.

- **Determination**: The quality of being determined: firmness of purpose; the process of establishing something exactly by calculation or research.

- **Dignity**: The state or quality of being worthy of honour or respect.

- **Direction**: A course along which someone moves in order to reach a destination.

- **Discovery**: Valuing the action or process of discovering.

- **Diversity**: A range of different things and situations.

- **Duty**: Moral obligation or responsibility.

- **Drive**: Personal source of power that provides the energy to set and keep in motion; move with great force.

- **Ease**: Make things happen more easily. Freedom from worries or problems. Absence of difficulty or effort.

- **Education**: The process of receiving or giving systematic instruction. Learning. Enlightening experiences.

- **Elegance**: Quality of being graceful and stylish in appearance or manner.

- **Empathy**: The ability to understand and share feelings and experiences of another.

- **Energy**: Strength, vitality, and sustaining a person's physical and mental powers.

- **Enjoyment**: The state or process of taking pleasure in something.

- **Enthusiasm**: Intense and eager enjoyment, interest or approval.

- **Ethics**: Moral principles that govern a person's behaviour.

- **Excellence**: The quality of being outstanding or extremely good.

- **Excitement**: A state of great enthusiasm and eagerness.

- **Expertise**: Skill or knowledge in a particular field or area.

- **Exploration**: Searching unfamiliar areas or thorough examination of subjects.

- **Fairness**: Impartial and just treatment or behaviour without discrimination.

- **Family**: People related to one and to be treated with a special loyalty or intimacy.

- **Fidelity**: Faithfulness to a person, cause or belief, demonstrated by continuing loyalty and support.

- **Financial freedom**: The power to spend wealth without restraint and with choice.

- **Fitness**: The condition of being physically fit and healthy.

- **Flow**: Proceed or be produced smoothly, continuously and effortlessly.

- **Focus**: The state of concentrating interest or activity on something.

- **Friendship**: State of mutual trust and support between people. A relationship between friends.

- **Freedom**: The power to act, speak or think as one wants without restraint and with choice.

- **Fun**: Enjoyment, amusement or light-hearted pleasure.

- **Gallantry**: Courageous behaviour.

- **Generosity**: The quality of being kind and generous.

- **Goodness**: The quality of being good and displaying moral excellence.

- **Grace**: Simple elegance or refinement of movement; courteous goodwill; an attractively polite manner of behaving.

- **Gratitude**: A quality of being thankful; readiness to show appreciation for and to return kindness.

- **Growth**: The process of developing or maturing physically, mentally or spiritually.

- **Happiness**: The state of being happy.

- **Harmony**: The quality of forming a pleasing and consistent whole.

- **Health**: A state of being well and free of illness or injury.

- **Honesty**: The quality of being honest.

- **Honour**: High respect; esteem. A person that brings credit.

- **Hope**: Grounds for believing that something good may happen. A feeling of expectation and desire for a certain thing to happen.

- **Humour**: The quality of being amusing or comic. The ability to express humour or make people laugh.

- **Humility**: An ability to keep a modest view of one's importance; humbleness.

- **Imagination**: The ability to form new ideas, images or concepts. To be creative and resourceful.

- **Independence**: The fact or state of being independent. Having control of thoughts and actions free of restriction.

- **Influence**: Capacity to have an effect on the character, development or behaviour of someone or something.

- **Ingenuity**: The quality of being clever, original and inventive.

- **Inner harmony**: Pleased with oneself physically, mentally and emotionally.

- **Inner peace**: A state of being at peace with oneself. Without emotional turmoil.

- **Insightfulness**: Having or showing an accurate and deep understanding; perceptive.

- **Inspiration**: A person or thing that inspires. The process of being mentally stimulated to do or feel something.

- **Integrity**: The quality of being honest and having strong moral principles; moral uprightness; a state of being whole and undivided.

- **Intimacy**: Close familiarity or friendship; closeness.

- **Intuition**: The ability to understand something immediately, without the need for a conscious reasoning.

- **Joy**: A feeling of great pleasure and happiness.

- **Justice**: The quality of being fair and reasonable.

- **Kindness**: The quality of being friendly, generous and considerate.

- **Knowledge**: The acquisition through experience and education of facts, information and skills. To be knowledgeable.

- **Leadership**: The state or position of being a leader. The action of leading people or an organisation.

- **Legacy**: Ideas, money, property left to someone or a group of people. A thing handed down by a predecessor.

- **Lifelong learning:** An ongoing desire for continuous learning for life.

- **Logic**: Reasoning conducted or assessed according to strict principles of validity.

- **Love**: An intense feeling of deep affection.

- **Loyalty**: The quality of being loyal to someone or something. A strong feeling of support or allegiance.

- **Making a difference**: Dedication to expanding the value that you offer and share with people or organisations.

- **Magic**: Influencing the course of events by using mysterious forces. State of seeing the 'majik' in the world.

- **Mastery**: Comprehensive knowledge or skill in a subject or accomplishment.

- **Mindfulness**: The quality or state of being conscious or aware of something. Consciously in the moment.

- **Motivation**: Desire or willingness to do something.

- **Mysteriousness**: Enjoying the difficult or impossible to consciously understand, explain or identify.

- **Nature**: The phenomena of the physical world collectively, including plants, animals, landscapes, and other features of the earth.

- **Neatness**: The quality or condition of being neat.

- **Openness**: Acceptance of or receptiveness to change or new ideas. A lack of restriction: accessibility.

- **Optimism**: Hopefulness and confidence about the future or the successful outcome of something.

- **Order**: A state in which everything is in its correct or appropriate place.

- **Organisation**: An efficient and orderly approach to tasks and life. The structure or arrangement of related or connected items.

- **Originality**: The quality of being novel or unusual. The ability to think independently and creatively.

- **Outrageousness**: Very bold, unusual and startling. Wildly exaggerated or improbable.

- **Partnership**: The state of being a partner or partners.

- **Patience**: The capacity to accept or tolerate delay, trouble or suffering without getting angry or upset.

- **Passion**: An intense desire or enthusiasm for something. A state or outburst of strong emotion.

- **Peace**: Mentally calm; serenity; quiet and tranquillity. Freedom from disturbance.

- **Persistence**: Firm continuance in a course of action in spite of difficulty or opposition.

- **Philanthropy**: Desire to promote the welfare of others by generous donation of time and/or money.

- **Playfulness**: Giving or expressing pleasure and amusement. Light-hearted.

- **Positivity**: Constructive in intention or attitude. Showing optimism and confidence.

- **Practicality**: A state of being practical. The aspects of a situation that involve the actual doing or experiencing of something.

- **Preparedness**: A state of readiness.

- **Professionalism**: The practising of an activity until a professional level is reached; not just amateur.

- **Quality**: The standard of something as measured against other things; the degree of excellence of something; general excellence of standard or level.

- **Recognition**: Appreciation or acclaim for an achievement, service or ability by self and others.

- **Relaxation**: State of rest and recreation free from tension and anxiety.

- **Reliability**: Consistently good in quality or performance; able to be trusted.

- **Reputation**: The beliefs or opinions that are generally held about you by others.

- **Respect**: State of being admired or respected.

- **Responsibility**: The state of having a duty to deal with something. Being accountable for something.

- **Resourcefulness**: Having the ability to find quick and clever ways to overcome difficulties.

- **Results-oriented**: Focused on outcomes of actions and projects.

- **Security**: State of safety or organisation and free of danger or threat.

- **Self-actualisation**: The realisation or fulfilment of one's talents and potentialities.

- **Self-control**: The ability to control one's emotions and desires or the expression of them.

- **Selflessness**: Concerned more with the needs and wishes of others than one's own. Unselfish.

- **Sensuality**: The enjoyment, expression or pursuit of physical, especially sexual, pleasure.

- **Serenity**: The state of being calm, peaceful and untroubled.

- **Service**: The action of helping, assisting or doing work for someone.

- **Sexiness**: Sexually attractive or exciting.

- **Sexuality**: A capacity for sexual feelings.

- **Simplicity**: The quality of being extremely easy to understand; plain, natural, simple.

- **Sincerity**: The quality of being free from pretence, deceit or hypocrisy.

- **Skilfulness**: Having or showing skill.

- **Spirituality**: Relating to, or affecting the human spirit or soul. Not concerned with material (physical) values or pursuits.

- **Spontaneity**: Condition of being spontaneous in behaviour or action.

- **Stability**: The state of being stable. Not likely to change; firmly established.

- **Status**: A relative social, professional or other standing of someone or something.

- **Stillness**: Deep silence and calm. Not moving or making a sound. Tranquil.

- **Strength**: The state of being strong. Physical power and energy.

- **Structure**: Constructing or arranging according to plan; giving a pattern or organisation to. The quality of being organised.

- **Success**: The attainment of a desired aim or purpose.

- **Support**: Give assistance, encouragement or emotional energy to people, causes or things.

- **Synergy**: The interaction or cooperation of two or more agents to produce a combined effect greater than the sum of their separate effects.

- **Teaching**: Sharing ideas or principles with others either formally or informally.

- **Teamwork**: Being involved in the combined action of a group of people, especially when effective and efficient.

- **Thankfulness**: Expressing gratitude. Pleased.

- **Thoughtfulness**: Showing consideration for the needs of other people.

- **Timeliness**: Done or occurring at a favourable or useful time; opportune.

- **Tolerance**: The ability or willingness to endure something, opinions or behaviour that one does not necessarily agree with.

- **Tradition**: Conducting aspects of life according to customs or beliefs passed down from generation to generation.

- **Tranquillity**: Quality or state of being calm, free of disturbance.

- **Transcendence**: Experience beyond the normal or physical level.

- **Trust**: Firm belief in the reliability, truth, ability or strength of someone or something.

- **Truth**: The quality or state of being true. A fact or belief that is true in accordance with fact or personal reality.

- **Understanding**: The ability to comprehend something. Intellect.

- **Uniqueness**: Being unlike anybody else, particularly remarkable, special or unusual.

- **Unity**: State of forming a complete and pleasing whole. Being joined as a whole.

- **Usefulness**: The quality or ability to be practical for a particular purpose.

- **Variety**: The state of being different or diverse.

- **Virtue**: A quality considered morally good or desirable in a person demonstrating behaviour showing high moral standards.

- **Vision**: The ability to think about or plan the future with imagination and/or wisdom.

- **Vitality**: The state of being strong and active; with energy.

- **Volunteering**: Working for an organisation without being paid.

- **Wellbeing**: State of being well on all levels: physically, mentally and emotionally.

- **Wealth**: State of being rich. Material prosperity. An abundance of valuable possessions or money.

- **Winning**: Gaining, resulting in, or relating to victory in a contest or competition. Attractive, endearing.

- **Wisdom**: The quality of having experience, knowledge and good judgement; the soundness of an action or decision with regard to the application of experience, knowledge and good judgement.

- **Wonder**: A state of awed admiration or respect.

- **Youthfulness**: Young or seeming young; a personal characteristic.

- **Zeal**: Great energy or enthusiasm in pursuit of a cause or an objective.

Now you have considered the list of values, choose your top ten. Don't worry about ranking them at this stage; just write down those that are most important to you from your CV and OV selections.

Allow yourself some time to do this. Many of my clients have fed back to me over the years that this can be quite hard as they sort through their options.

As mentioned at the start of this wealth section, I suggest being Self-ish here, as you really think about what is important to you at this time. Go with your gut – there doesn't have to be a logical reason when it comes to the values that are important to you.

My Top 10 Life Values *(in no particular order)*:

Value #1: _____

Value #2: _____

Value #3: _____

Value #4: _____

Value #5: _____

Value #6: _____

Value #7: _____

Value #8: _____

Value #9: _____

Value #10: _____

Once you have your top ten values, the next exercise is to rank those values in order of importance at this particular point in time.

Start by asking yourself: If I could choose only one value from my list of ten, which one would it be? This may take some thinking... go for it now!

My Top 10 Life Values
(in order from most important to least important):

Value #1: _____

Value #2: _____

Value #3: _____

Value #4: _____

Value #5: _____

Value #6: _____

Value #7: _____

Value #8: _____

Value #9: _____

Value #10: _____

Congratulations! Welcome to a new world of understanding and insight into who you are and what is important to you. Very few people on the planet are consciously aware of and clear on their values.

Your values can become a strong and conscious guide for activities that you might do, moving forward, in all the wealth areas that are being explored in this book.

It means you are taking actions and making decisions that are in your best interests and you know why they are important to you. The next section will delve deeper into this. The real point is that you start to own what you do and you do it with an underlying purpose. This is a very empowering process.

It's important to understand and appreciate that, over time, your values may change. Values evolve over the course of your life. Different things are important to, say, somebody who's just finished their education compared to someone in midlife with young children. Similarly, different things are important to someone looking at leaving full-time employment. That uniqueness is yours; hold on to it. Hold on to what's important to you right now and revisit your list often, to see if things may have changed.

The most important thing about this exercise is that the values you've selected belong to you, as do the definitions. You own your values. And owning your values is the key to really owning your life moving forward.

All of my clients complete this exercise. Within a few weeks, they are able to articulate what is important to them and why they have started to integrate some routines into their weekly activities. The one that stands out for me is the man who listed family in his top three values. When pressed, he revealed that he wanted to be as active as possible with his grandchildren for as long as possible. As a result, he realised that he needed to exercise on a regular basis in order to be able to keep pace with the kids. Before doing this exercise, fitness had been in his SV (Sometimes Valued) space. Afterwards, it moved to the top ten because it was important for living a higher value. He had both reason and purpose to maintain and improve his fitness. Powerful!

We are going to move on to beliefs next. It's important to have supporting and assisting beliefs that are in alignment with your values. Why? In order for you to act on any of the values that you have identified above, you must also believe in that value. Where there is a disconnect between a value and an associated belief, little or no action will take place. In some cases, the disconnect can make activities more stressful than they need to be. When you are clear on your values and you have beliefs that are in alignment with them, then what you can achieve and the feeling of enjoyment you can experience on the journey forward is amazing.

YOUR BELIEFS

My friend was passing the elephants in a sanctuary when he suddenly stopped, confused by the fact that these huge creatures were being held only by a small rope tied to their front leg. No chains, no cages. It was obvious that the elephants could, at any time, break away from the ropes they were tied to, but, for some reason, they did not. My friend saw a trainer nearby and asked why these beautiful, magnificent animals just stood there and made no attempt to get away.

'Well,' he said, 'when they are very young and much smaller, we use the same size rope to tie them and, at that age, it's enough to hold them. As they grow up, they are conditioned to believe they cannot break away. They believe the rope can still hold them, so they never try to break free.'

My friend was amazed. These animals could, at any time, break free from their bonds, but because they believed they couldn't, they were stuck right where they were.

Beliefs are our way of BE-ing in the world. They are the way we see the world, the way that we uniquely experience it.

Some of our beliefs are useful and some of our beliefs may not be so useful at this particular point in time.

In a nutshell, our beliefs are the rules that we live by, consciously or unconsciously. What we want to create are rules that are in alignment with and that support and assist us to live our values. So let's have a look at beliefs in the general sense.

The rules that we live by can come from many different sources, including the many experiences we have had in our past.

Often, the rules we live by (and the values we live by) have been installed in us over a long period of time and imprinted at a very young age. Beliefs that our parents, grandparents, school, community, religion and society have set for us, even though we may not have had a conscious say in the installation of those beliefs.

One example of an installed belief might come from your grandparents, who experienced the Great Depression as kids and saw their parents go through a world of pain and poverty. Growing up, you may have heard them tell you time and time again that life is tough. It is probably what your parents would have heard over and over.

Without even knowing it, you have a strongly held belief about the world that colours your perception of it. It has been installed in you. Holding the world view that life is tough, you are more likely to see in day-to-day life that it *is* tough. Tough for you, tough for the people you see in public, tough for the people you see on TV. Your focus is your reality. It becomes your experience.

Focus on what you DO want rather than what you don't want when creating supporting beliefs.

Here are some examples of installed beliefs:

Work – Many of my clients over the years have come out of the resources and construction industries. They have a strongly held belief in the concept of 'Zero Harm' – the idea that every employee gets home safely, 'takes five' (takes five seconds to observe the environment), and adheres to strict workplace health and safety policies and practices

School – We learn in school that you must obey all the rules or there are consequences. Going against the rules means getting in trouble, such as being awarded detention or losing privileges. Any behaviour contrary to the rules of the establishment is WRONG. Although seen as unacceptable in the 21st century, students were once often punished by strap and cane for breaking the rules in school. For many, the rules they lived by at school have been imprinted and have become unconscious beliefs – beliefs that are often never explored or questioned. At this time in life, some of these beliefs may not be all that useful.

Religion – Now, I'm not here to comment on the credence of any one religion, but I will point out that religions around the world serve to provide great examples of installed beliefs. Take, for example:

- In Christianity: The Ten Commandments;
- In Islam: The Six Major Beliefs;
- In Buddhism: The Three Universal Truths and Four Noble Truths;
- In Hinduism: The teachings that…
  - The Vedas are the ultimate authority;
  - Everyone should strive to achieve dharma;
  - Individual souls are immortal; and
  - The goal of the individual soul is Moksha (liberation).

A quick and simple example of a disconnect between someone's values and their beliefs is around money.

Say my value is financial freedom, but when I have a look at my beliefs around finances and wealth I find out, when I dig deep enough, that I believe 'money is the root of all evil' or 'money doesn't grow on trees'. There is a direct disconnect between the value of financial freedom and those beliefs; I'm not going to help myself to live in financial freedom if I believe it's wrong or difficult to have or amass money.

At this stage, what I need to think about is what type of belief would be in alignment with my value of financial freedom.

Take the belief: *'Money comes easily and frequently and from ever increasing sources.'*

Now, THAT is a useful belief to support financial freedom as a value.

Since this book is about wealth beyond money, below are some more examples:

WELLBEING

My value is wellbeing: the state of being well on all levels – physically, mentally and emotionally.

When I explore my beliefs around wellbeing, I find that, deep down, I believe it is a lot of hard work, and that true wellbeing in every aspect of life is impossible to attain.

Here, there is once again a clear disconnect between what my value is and what I believe. I need to create a belief that is going to support my wellbeing.

At the beginning a good supporting belief may be: 'Wellbeing is important to me and it is possible. Each day I do one thing that leads me to wellbeing.'

In time, this belief might turn into: 'I am living my definition of wellbeing every day.'

Some beliefs need to evolve over time, changing gradually. It is very hard to go from being fifteen kilos overweight, enjoying chocolate and take-away food, to being in a state of total wellbeing. Like the medical professional who went from full-on full-time employment to full-on nothing and fell off the retirement cliff emotionally, our body and mind need time to adjust to changes.

OPTIMISM

My value is optimism: hopefulness and confidence about the future or the successful outcome of something.

When I explore my beliefs, I find that, deep down, I believe that bad things happen to good people. Most of my self-talk is cautious, focused on what might happen in the negative and based on a fear of the future. I often think along the lines of: I want this to happen, BUT what if… then…

The change that I need to happen here is a simple one; however, it may take some time to effect.

The supporting belief could be: 'I believe good things happen to good people. I am deservedly optimistic about the future and my success in all areas of my life.'

Simple but effective.

Having and, where necessary, creating beliefs in alignment with our values, we have a very effective tool to start to measure how we are going now and into the future in terms of living our lives.

The next exercise encourages you to build empowering beliefs behind each of your values.

Exercise: Embracing Empowering and Supporting Beliefs

Take each of your top ten values in turn and identify an underlying supporting belief for each one.

VALUE #1: _____

Supporting belief #1:

_____

_____

VALUE #2: _____

Supporting belief #2:

_____

_____

VALUE #3: _____

Supporting belief #3:

_____

_____

VALUE #4: _____

Supporting belief #4:

_____

_____

VALUE #5: _____

Supporting belief #5:

_____

_____

VALUE #6: _____

Supporting belief #6:

_____

_____

VALUE #7: _____

Supporting belief #7:

_____

_____

VALUE #8: _____

Supporting belief #8:

_____

_____

VALUE #9: _____

Supporting belief #9:

_____

_____

VALUE #10: _____

Supporting belief #10:

_____

_____

So how do you adopt these new beliefs instead of any limiting beliefs that may have been in place? Without the use of hypnosis or putting you in a deep trance, the replacement of limiting beliefs with more empowering beliefs is a matter of repetition and association that moves from conscious incompetence to conscious competence and finally into unconscious competence.

The best way to consider the process of integration of new beliefs is to think about the time you learnt to drive a car. In the beginning, the process of driving a car takes a lot of energy. It doesn't feel natural. You need to think through every move your body makes and follow the instructions of your teacher. At first, driving is a chore. It's clunky. Most of us will have stalled and bunny-hopped our way to getting around the car park, paddock or wide, low-traffic road to begin with. However, over time, you get to know exactly how to drive while being aware of what is happening around you. Eventually, almost unconsciously, the process becomes easy. Then, unless something is out of place, you don't need to think about driving. In fact, you can drive, listen to the radio and be on automatic pilot. Some people even get to a stage of unconscious competence, where if you asked what happened around them as they drove to work in the morning, they wouldn't be able to remember the details of the trip.

A similar process occurs when you develop empowering beliefs. At first, when you read them (preferably aloud), they seem 'unreal' – uncomfortable and clunky. Through repetition and refinement, there comes a point where you feel comfortable with the new belief. Eventually, you well and truly believe it. Your beliefs come in alignment with your values. Your experience then reinforces your beliefs, and so it continues.

Now we've considered your values and beliefs, we're going to turn to your wellbeing.

2. Wellbeing

'For everyone, wellbeing is a journey.
The secret is committing to that journey and taking those
first steps with hope and belief.'

— DEEPAK CHOPRA

QUESTIONS TO CONSIDER IN THIS PART OF THE BOOK:
- How can I improve my nutrition?
- How can I improve my fitness?
- How can I improve my mental health?

There's an old saying: Health equals wealth. As a next-ager, this is truer than at any other time of your life.

Certainly, health is one of the wealth areas we have the opportunity to embrace in our lives moving forward. The choices we make along the way make all the difference.

Health can be broken up into several areas. I'm not going to preach in this section, just touch base with the bare essentials that make the difference between leaving full-time work successfully and setting yourself up for post-work depression.

We're going to cover the following aspects:

- Food and nutrition
- Physical fitness
- Mental health

The below diagram illustrates the difference in paths between those who are in optimal health for their age and those who are in poor health for their age (thanks to J Herrmann for the graphic):

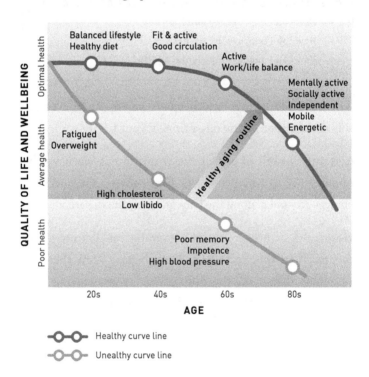

As we get older, it naturally takes more planning and effort to stay in good shape. The good news is that when you leave full-time work, you have more time available to pursue fitness and other health goals. With the eight to twelve extra hours per day that used to be taken up by work-related activities now at your disposal, you can't fall back on old excuses, such as, 'There's just not enough time to exercise,' or 'There's not enough time to shop and cook.' You can take control of your wellbeing.

Staying fit and healthy is a major prerequisite for accomplishing what you want to do in other areas of your life. The old adage 'Discipline can set you free,' certainly rings true in this wealth area of your life. Former professional golfer Greg Norman is a great example who, as part of his weekly routine, spends up to two hours a day in the gym and has a strict eating regime to maintain his wellbeing.

Many pre-planned and eagerly anticipated 'next stage' trips and events have been ruined by lack of health rather than lack of funds. You may have lots of money to invest in travel, but if you have difficulty walking, you're not going make the hike up Mt Kilimanjaro or even be able to stroll around your locality pain free.

Poor health can also force you out of your desired housing into accommodation where you require daily assistance. You've probably heard it before, but now you're going to hear it from me. You need to focus on your wellbeing as a whole.

Three key health areas you have control over during the next stage of your life are diet, exercise and stress. Let's look at each area to see what you can do to optimise your health. Some of you will begin anew as you transition into the next stage of your life; others will continue with what you have already been doing. Even if you're already health conscious, it's worth revisiting the basics.

FOOD AND NUTRITION

A good friend of mine in his late forties has a very simple test for the food going into his body.

He puts food into two categories:

1. Beneficial to my health; or
2. Going to kill me.

Each time he consumes food, he asks himself, 'Is this beneficial for my health or is it going to kill me?' And then he proceeds accordingly. He figures if his percentage is eighty per cent beneficial food and twenty per cent bad food, he'll do well over the many years he plans to be on the planet.

For most people, eating happens anywhere up to six times a day. So, on average, every few hours, our attention is on food. The decisions we make in order to determine what goes into our mouths can be good for us or bad for us. Either way, it has an effect on our overall health, increasingly so the older we get.

What you eat has a huge influence on whether you are a prime candidate for high or low blood pressure, heart attacks and a multitude of other diseases and illnesses in older life. So it's worth minimising these risks.

Some of you reading this will already have pretty good eating habits. However, if you are like most people, you won't. Your habits may need some serious modification. And this can be harder work than you think. Cold turkey changes do not generally work for most people. It's about becoming more conscious about what you eat and making a good call on the types of food you put into your body.

Where possible, it's best to refine your favourite treats and reduce how frequently you enjoy them over time. Once you get into a new habit of avoiding one food, you will find it easier to move on to another food that may not be so good for you.

Whatever you do, consult your local nutritionist, dietitian, doctor or other health professional before you make any big changes.

'To know and not to do is really not to know.'

— STEVE COVEY

A simple rule to follow is: reduce fat, processed sugar and salt. But how can you go about this?

Less Processed Sugar

- In a nutshell, use less processed sugar (white, brown, raw) and syrups in your food, drinks and recipes.

- For snacks, eat fruit (apples, mandarins, grapes, etc.), vegetables (carrots, celery, etc.), plain natural yoghurt and whole-grain crackers, rather than chocolate, biscuits, cakes and ice cream.

- Drink water and natural (not processed) fruit juices instead of soft drinks and hot drinks with added sugar.

- Use stevia/natvia/Xylitol or naturally occurring sweeteners (not sweetening chemicals) in tea and coffee.

- Eat fresh fruit or fruits canned in their own juice, not in heavy syrup.

Less Fat

- Eat mainly fruit, vegetables, fish, poultry (without the skin), pulses and peas for higher protein intake.

- Eat leaner cuts of red meat and trim off excess fat (this can be hard to do because it tastes so great).

- Eat eggs (two or three per week); however, increase egg whites if you prefer.

- Limit intake of dairy products such as cream, chocolate and cheeses.

- Grill, roast, steam or boil foods, rather than fry, and use a rack to drain excess fat when possible.

Less Salt

- Where possible, consider cooking without salt and look for alternatives, such as seasoning food with lemon, spices and herbs.

- Reduce the salty foods you eat, including canned soups, potato chips, salted nuts, cheese, processed meats, and condiments such as soy sauce, tomato sauce, barbecue sauce, ketchup and garlic salt.

- Eat nuts, fresh fruit and vegetables.

- Check packet ingredients for salt (sodium), monosodium glutamate (aka MSG) or any other man-made food additives, and other artificial food enhancers, and avoid products containing high levels of any of them.

Well, this is all easier said than done, isn't it?!

Why, for so many of us, is it so difficult to make and stick to these changes?

There are a few reasons for this. We've come to see a lot of sweet food as comfort food, and changing habits built over a long period of time is not easy. It doesn't help that today's marketing campaigns in the food industry muddy the waters when it comes to the connection between foods and their ingredients and health and wellbeing.

At the end of the day, the way to be successful in changing old and maybe not-so-useful habits is by gradual integration.

As you progress adding and substituting healthier foods for the old foods, you'll find new foods that will be satisfying to you. If you can see this process as part of a bigger picture of greater health, wellbeing and increased energy, then it makes the process worthwhile.

As Deepak Chopra reveals in the opening quote to this chapter, wellbeing is a journey. A start to that journey can be achieved in the exercise below.

Exercise: Food Audit

Do a food and drink audit: think about what you have eaten and what you have had to drink in the past two weeks.

While you think about it, write it down or tap it out into a Word document. Include everything. Also include roughly (or precisely) how much you consumed of each food or drink.

Once you have brain dumped and have everything down, including the amounts, use the simple qualification:

1. Is this food or drink beneficial for my health?
2. Will this food or drink kill me?

Pick your top five beneficial foods or drinks and your top five killers.

Now put in place a plan to increase your ratio of beneficial food and drink to less beneficial food and drink. Make the reductions in particular in a slow fashion. It could take a few months to get to a level that is sustainable.

Here is an example:

Top 5 foods and drinks that will benefit me	Plans, strategies and actions moving forward
1. Water	Drink often through the day. Carry water with me on my travels.
2. Salads	Have salad with over-the-counter meals rather than French fries. Learn to love different salads.
3. Proteins	Educate myself more on various proteins and the amounts to eat for optimal wellbeing.
4. Nuts and Grains	Increase my nut and dried fruit mixes and intake for snacks during a week.
5. Prunes/Psyllium Husk	Add to meals for overall and colonic health. Keep clearing the tubes.

Top 5 foods and drinks that will kill me	Plans, strategies and actions moving forward
1. Chocolate	Instead of eating the whole bar, I'll eat ½ a bar each time or share the chocolate offering.
2. Alcohol	Drink alcohol only on Fridays/Saturdays and Sundays and have at least 4 alcohol-free days each week. Volunteer to be designated driver more often.
3. Excessive coffee (over 4 cups per day)	Aim to have only 2 coffees per day except Sundays. Drink and experiment with more herbal infusions for hot drinks.
4. Take away and fast food	Have 4 fast food meals each month instead of 8. Choose healthier fast food options. Eat only ½ the deep fried chips that I receive.
5. Sugar	Use other forms of natural stevia-based sweeteners.

Okay, now it's your turn...

Top 5 foods and drinks that will benefit me	Plans, strategies and actions moving forward
1.	
2.	
3.	
4.	
5.	

Top 5 foods and drinks that will kill me	Plans, strategies and actions moving forward
1.	
2.	
3.	
4.	
5.	

Great effort! By unpacking your head and putting this on paper, you are now more aware when it comes to what's going into your body. Now follow up that awareness with action!

If you are like most people I have met, changing habits and creating a new routine can take some effort. I suggest aiming for eighty per cent compliance with your new plan rather than trying to stick to it totally and completely. Endeavour to have some fun with it as well. Try new things! Over time, the benefits to your overall health and wellbeing will be marked. And if you slip up, don't beat yourself up about it; you don't want to be stressed while undertaking this process – you just want to be aware. Awareness is much better than nothing.

The next area to think about is fitness. But it's worth keeping in mind that you can't out-exercise a bad diet. The different aspects of your health and wellbeing need to be in balance; the different areas need to support each other.

FITNESS

Let's be clear right from the start. While, for some of you, exercise is an integral part of life, for others it is not. Either way, you don't have to be a Super Senior to experience the benefits of exercise.

I'm not talking about becoming a fitness freak with a hardcore workout regime. For most men, a moderate exercise program is just what the doctor ordered. It's easier to implement, it is more pleasurable, and there's less risk of injury. You don't get fitter by being injured and in pain all the time and you don't want to begin the next stage of your life in such a way.

There are three major types of exercise:

- Aerobic and Endurance: Running, jogging, trekking, cycling, swimming, dancing and any sustained exercise that raises your heart rate and generates energy is considered aerobic. In a gym setting, this could include interval training, spin classes, rowing machines, treadmills, climbing machines, etc.

- Stretching/Flexibility: Examples include yoga, Pilates and calisthenics/warm-up exercises.

- Building Strength: Weight training and lifting.

Ideally, you should incorporate all three into your exercise program. Your health professional can assist you to develop an effective and safe exercise program – one that is custom made for you.

But it's okay to start small. The main thing to recognise is that building some sort of exercise into your daily and weekly routine means consciously making time for it. There are small strategies that you can consciously employ in order to remain active. Instead of driving everywhere, for example, you may choose to ride a bike or walk to your destination. Take the stairs instead of lifts in shopping centres and when visiting friends.

At the most basic level, regardless of your current fitness level, thirty to forty-five minutes walking three or four times a week will keep you in basic order.

My stepfather is eighty-four and goes to the gym three to five times a week. Does he love it? No. However, he is aware that if he doesn't, he will not be able to play with the grandkids, and he will not be able to keep up with my mother, who is over a decade younger than him. To him, the benefits of *being* fit far outweigh the negatives of *getting* fit. It is a commitment and one he keeps. It is part of his routine.

Exercise over the long term will maintain and strengthen the internal organs that are reliant on muscles, such as your heart and lungs. The ultimate aim is to slow the rate of physical and mental deterioration that is part of getting older.

Fitness Facts

This section is about presenting you with some facts you may be unaware of. Working on your awareness is a big part of being able to access the wealth in this area of life – extending your life into the bargain! I'm not trying to teach you to suck eggs; even if you're well aware of these things, it's really worth the reminder.

1. For every decade that you are on the planet, your heart's ability to pump blood around the body reduces by about eight per cent.

2. On average, an adult man will lose between three and five per cent of their muscle tissue with each decade of life.

3. At age seventy-five, you will be using and processing fifty per cent less oxygen than you did when you were twenty-five (fifty years younger).

4. Stretching keeps your muscles and joints from stiffening up and causing ongoing aches and pains. It increases your body's general flexibility.

5. Tiring, low impact exercise during the day (such as walking, bike riding or swimming) can assist you to sleep better.

6. There is a strong biological connection between physical health and mental health.

7. If you are physically fit, you look and feel better. You're toned and your physical appearance is enhanced. Simple fact!

8. Exercise helps to reduce your appetite right after you have completed your workout.

9. Exercise releases useless emotions and relieves other stresses and anxieties.

10. Exercise creates a sense of general wellbeing.

It's important to connect the benefits of exercise with your ongoing health, otherwise people tend not to take action.

Exercise: Future Fitness

Create a vision of your future fitness in three or five years. Use the series of questions presented here to help you.

This is what a future fitness vision might look like:

I eat a balanced combination of foods that I tailor for my own health and wellbeing.

This includes whole natural foods such as:

- *Salads – including garden, Caesar (no anchovies and little cream sauce), Greek, mixed, Thai, feta, pesto, coleslaw, Asian and herb salads.*

- *Proteins – eggs, chicken, fish, lean beef and lamb, seafood, pork, cheese (moderately), turkey and natural yoghurts.*

- *Nuts and grains – almonds, oats, pistachios, cashews.*

I drink lots of water.

I do indulge every now and then. And I really enjoy it when I do.

I detoxify periodically, including juice and mono-fruit (grapes) fasting.

I drink alcohol moderately for enjoyment and appreciation.

I am conscious of foods that may kill me and I eat them in moderation.

My health is excellent physically and energetically on all levels.

I exercise four times a week, including a personal training session and a mix of walking, gym sessions, interval training, yoga classes and Pilates sessions.

I weigh 71kg and have a waist measurement of 89cm. I look and feel great. I am staying young. I am healthy and fit.

Here are some questions to consider as you build your own future fitness vision:

- What do you like to eat that is healthy?

- What do you need to eat more of? Less of?

- What do you need to drink more of? Less of?

- What would you prefer to weigh? What is your recommended weight range?

- What is your recommended stomach circumference range?

- What exercise do you need to take to achieve your desired results?

- What activities would you like to be able to do (e.g. touch your toes, lift weights, play with grandkids, walk and trek overseas, etc.)?

MENTAL AND EMOTIONAL WELLBEING

There is little doubt that mental and emotional health is one of the dominant 21st century issues. Hardly a week goes by without reference in the popular press or online to the different groups within our society, old and young, who are being touched by mental and emotional health issues.

As a next-ager moving out of full-time work and into the next stage of your life, it is worth spending some time considering what causes you stress.

In the first part of the book, we explored change using Bridges' Model and we looked at some of the emotions that are involved, such as denial, anxiety, shock, fear, anger, frustration and confusion. Stress is clearly a part of change. In this case, the life changes associated with moving from full-time work and into the next stage of your life can be stressful.

It is important to acknowledge that it is natural for human beings to experience stress in times of great change. So the question becomes: How can you tell if you are experiencing mental and emotional health issues?

If not dealt with, and in its worst form, stress can present as depression. At the back of the book in the appendix is a Depression Symptoms Checklist that may be of use to you in this time of change.

It is important to recognise that there is both positive stress and negative stress. Positive stress, also known as good stress or eustress, motivates you. It can move you towards your goals and is perceived as having a good outcome, e.g. exercising or anticipating an upcoming event like a wedding, birthday party or holiday.

In contrast, negative stress, or distress, has a negative impact on you mentally and emotionally. It detracts from your general wellbeing. Negative stress can be:

- Time-sensitive (e.g. being late to an appointment);
- Anticipating a stressful event (e.g. public speaking, if you don't enjoy it);
- Situational (e.g. a car accident); or
- Due to an encounter (e.g. unexpectedly bumping into an ex-partner).

Being aware of both positive and negative stressors in your next stage of life makes it easier to include the good and reduce the bad.

In times of change, it does take time to adjust the mind, body and soul. For some, it can take a week, for some a month, for others a year. Some take even longer. Ultimately, what's important is awareness around how you are doing and how you are feeling. It's important to understand that feelings of fear, anger, frustration and confusion are a natural part of the change process and don't mean that you're going crazy.

So, when you *are* expressing stress in your life, what do you do about it?

One of the keys to mental and emotional wellbeing is understanding how you deal with stress. Below are some ideas for you to explore.

We're going to go through several effective tools and techniques for coping with and managing stress. You may already do other things that work well for you. That's great! Continue to use what works and regard the following list as possible additions to your tool kit.

SHARE: TALK IT OUT; DON'T STUFF IT IN!

- Find people you trust and respect. Talk to them about your problems. This frequently relieves stress, and you may gain new perspectives that lead to creative solutions.

- Talk to others about *their* problems, too. Sometimes hearing what's happening to others puts your issues in perspective. Men's sheds and other men's groups can be of assistance.

- Seek professional assistance from your GP, a therapist or a counsellor.

- Some companies will let previous employees access their Employee Assistance Program for some months after they have left full-time employment.

THINK: SOLUTION-FINDING AND PROBLEM-SOLVING IS AN ANTIDOTE TO STRESS

- Eliminate distorted or irrational thinking. Take note of thoughts such as: 'Other people don't care about me,' 'I'm over the hill,' 'I'll never be able to compete with my skill level,' etc. Once you catch yourself with these thoughts, one strategy to deal with them is to ask yourself: 'Is this thought (or thinking) useful at this time?' If the answer is 'no', think of something more useful. Picture something that makes you smile or feel good. If you find that negative thinking is happening quite a bit, then here's a strategy to break your thought loop: keep a rubber band around your wrist to act as a pattern interrupt. When you're having negative thoughts, lift it and let it rebound, giving you a sting.

- Analyse recurring sources of stress to determine how you can break the cycle. Many of us fill our lives with additional sources of stress, creating expectations either of others or ourselves that are unrealistic. In many cases, by deciding which tasks or responsibilities are more important, we can gain more control over our schedules.

- Analyse the situations and people that stress you out, and avoid them. The effort you put into this analysis goes a long way towards reducing stress. This is easier to do in social situations than in work situations. You can't always avoid stressful people and situations completely, but analyse the biggest stress creators and think about ways to minimise them. There may be ways you can collaborate with others to reduce both your stress and theirs.

SWEAT: EXERCISE FOR IMMEDIATE POSITIVE RESULTS!

- Get regular exercise. This releases pent-up anxiety and strengthens the body, enabling you to better withstand stress. Whatever you're doing now, do more!

- Plan enjoyable physical activities. These increase positive stress and decrease negative stress.

- Walk more. Both planned walks and impromptu walks are beneficial (for example, parking in the back of the parking lot and walking farther to the store).

ORGANISE: PLAN AND MANAGE YOUR DAY

- As it says on one of my many notebooks: WRITE SH*T DOWN! When under stress, it is common to lose track of the little details, like appointments and other commitments. Get a planner system that works for you and use it. Most phones and computers have good calendar software included nowadays.

- Plan enjoyable activities.

- Adopt a less stressful schedule. It is often possible to travel, do your banking and shopping, and pursue leisure and other activities during the less frenetic, off-peak hours.

- Get enough sleep. A rested mind and body can better handle stress.

- Follow a well-balanced, nutritious diet. This strengthens the body, enabling you to better handle stress. A poor or unbalanced diet stresses the body.

- Choose to stop striving for perfection. People who have unrealistic expectations for their own performance subject themselves to tremendous pressure. Find opportunities to go easier on yourself. Focus less on achieving perfect results and more on the enjoyment of whatever you choose to pursue.

- Choose to act happy. Exhibiting cheerful behaviour, even when you don't feel cheerful, often fools the rest of the body's systems into reducing stress reactions.

- Choose to soothe. Use relaxation techniques. Progressive relaxation, massage, meditation and yoga are just a few of the techniques available that relax the mind and body. Purchase relaxation tapes for this purpose.

- Choose positive self-talk. The voices in our own heads that judge and criticise what we do create negative self-talk. Catch yourself and replace those comments with affirmations.

- Choose to take a breath. Breathing deeply keeps the oxygen flowing and relaxes your muscles (see below in 7 Ancient Principles of Wellbeing).

- Choose to laugh. Belly laughs reduce your pulse and blood pressure for up to forty minutes.

TAKE ACTION: DEVISE A STRESS MANAGEMENT ACTION PLAN

Having an action plan to use when you feel overwhelmed is a very powerful way to combat fear, frustration, confusion and stress. This maps what you are going to do before getting into situations where you know you won't be able to think clearly.

Record actions or events that you know are stressors for you and devise a coping strategy to adhere to once you're in the midst of things.

For example:

Stressor: Family Christmas

Coping Strategy: Conscious time-out. Take a break for twenty minutes after Christmas lunch and make an ice run to the petrol station.

7 ANCIENT PRINCIPLES OF WELLBEING

Before we move on, I want to share with you seven ancient principles of wellbeing. Adapted from work done by Don Tolman, Anthony Robbins and others, this guidance will help you cultivate your health and wellbeing in general, whether or not you are faced with specific stresses and strains.

1. AIR AND BREATHING

Natural flowing air is good for you, so open a window or two. Vitality will follow.

Deep diaphragm breathing (as opposed to shallow chest breathing) is an ancient tradition that can oxygenate your blood and help you feel great.

The ratio of 1:4:2 usually works well. To start with, breathe in for three seconds, hold your breath for twelve seconds, then release it over the next six seconds. Work up to breathing in for seven seconds, holding for twenty-eight, and breathing out for fourteen. Repeat this exercise five times and do it three times a day. You'll notice the difference in your energy levels. If the 1:4:2 ratio doesn't work well for you, then try the very simple 4:8:8 ratio: Breathe in for four seconds, hold it for eight seconds and breathe out for eight seconds. This does wonders for your physiology.

2. WATER

The Ancients knew all about water; they drank lots of H_2O.

Modern science also tells us that ninety per cent of all headaches are caused by de-hydration; nothing more, nothing less.

At least 1.5 litres of water a day will keep you hydrated and allow your body to remove toxins. While a few more toilet stops may be required, the long-term benefits well outweigh the short-term inconvenience.

3. SUNSHINE

Sunshine is good for you. Various studies show that many people today are vitamin D deficient; in other words, they are pale and pasty looking anaemic. The most natural source of vitamin D is sunshine.

Ancient civilizations had no sunscreen but they did have common sense. What they saw in nature was that the combination of sun and water allowed all their plants and food to grow in abundance. Without one, the other would not occur. The question is: Why are humans any different? The answer is: We are not. We need natural sunlight the same as any organism on the face of the planet. The Ancients knew this so they made time to be in the sun for their health. They played outdoors and they also worked outdoors.

Over the centuries, different skin tones appeared, adapting to the environment. While some skin colours can absorb more sun than others, all humans need exposure to natural sunlight for health and vitality.

So, get out into the sunshine for half an hour a day (choose your hours carefully). You can combine this with walking, the next principle of health and wellbeing.

4. **WALKING**

Forty-five minutes walking, at pace, four times a week is enough to maintain a reasonable level of fitness and wellbeing. One of the simplest forms of depression eradication is to get up and walk at a quick pace for several minutes, keeping your eyeline above the horizon. Why? Because walking changes your physiology. It increases your heart rate, which, in turn, stimulates the release of serotonin and endorphins throughout your body. Both chemicals do one thing for you – they make you feel good.

5. WHOLE, NATURAL FOODS

Our human bodies are a reflection of the natural world around us, and foods are a great example.

There is a close connection and relationship between the visual look of foods and the areas they affect in our physical bodies. It is called the Law or Doctrine of Signatures. One of the best examples is the carrot. Slice across a carrot and you will notice that it looks a lot like an eye. Science has proven the consumption of carotene has a positive effect on the operation of one's eyes. Hence the old lesson that if you eat lots of carrots, you'll be able to see in the dark.

Another example is the humble walnut. When you look at a walnut, it looks very similar to a human brain. Research cited in the *Journal of Alzheimer's Disease* found that patients who ate walnuts had improved brain function and memory.

The Ancients knew the value of wholefoods and would often use them to treat symptoms of illness.

The Law of Signatures is fascinating and I could go on and on about it; however, the real point here is to eat, when possible and as part of your food plan moving forward, as much fresh and whole/natural/organic (there were no pesticides in ancient times) produce as you possibly can each day, each week, each year.

Remember: What you eat today walks and talks tomorrow.

6. NON-TOXIC RELATIONSHIPS

The Ancients were very aware that not all relationships are good for our ongoing wellbeing. It might be worth conducting a relationship review with all the people in your life. From family to friends, and from work to recreation relationships, bring into your awareness those which are the most pleasing and those which are the most difficult relationships to maintain in your life.

Relationships that, by and large, make you happy and feel good are non-toxic (though this doesn't mean you won't have disagreements along the way – it's only natural). Other relationships are toxic. These drain your personal energy, your life force, chi or manha – your BE-ing. Choose to have in your circle of friends, associates and relatives only those who are positive, optimistic, curious and generally happy. Also consider the kind of relationship you have with yourself; this is the most important relationship of all.

7. PASSION

The Ancients believed and today's science is now proving (through long-term studies at Yale and Harvard Business School, for example) that people who live with passion in their lives can live up to eighteen years longer than those who do not. Why? Because human beings without purpose, hope or a sense of gratitude have very little to live for or look forward to. They don't live; they exist.

The key here is to avoid what I call VCS – Vertical Coffin Syndrome. As one of my clients put it, 'Keep me away from places of the living dead.'

So, what are you passionate about? Let passion be your compass and then pass your passion on to others. This is the essence of BE-ing an inspirational person.

The pop rock band New Radicals sang at the end of last century, 'You get what you give,' and so it is in life.

A lot of information has been covered in this chapter. The seven ancient principles of wellbeing provide a great place to start making positive changes to your life in a simple way.

So embrace the seven principles and be aware of the three aspects of your wellbeing: food and nutrition; fitness; and mental and emotional wellbeing. Treasure your health – it truly is one of your greatest sources of fulfilment.

3. Location, Location, Location

'Home is not a place... It's a feeling.'

— CECILIA AHERN

QUESTIONS TO CONSIDER IN THIS SECTION:

- **Where will I be happiest? And why?**
- **Whom do I need to have conversations with about moving?**
- **Is it a good time to downsize?**

This wealth area is about where you want to live during the next stage of your life.

I consider location a wealth beyond money because when you get it right, it has the potential to enhance all other aspects of your life.

You've probably heard the old saying from the real estate and commercial industries: 'Location, location, location.' If you have the flexibility to have three houses – great! You might plan to split your time between them over the course of a year. For many, however, this may not be an option, so where you make your home in the next stage of your life can become an issue. The right move has the power to provide you with much joy, fun and fulfilment, while the wrong one can do the opposite.

There are many benefits to choosing the correct location. These can include: closer and more frequent connection with loved ones and friends, a great lifestyle, new adventures, a new start, simplification of life (via downsizing), being walking distance to the beach and having access to top local restaurants, sporting facilities, entertainment and shopping precincts. The list goes on…

The important thing to remember here is there is no one right answer. There's no magic formula that I can give you in these pages for selecting the one (or two or three or more) place that's right for you and the people close to you.

One of the shortest programs I have ever conducted lasted two sessions. It was with a gentleman whose role had been made redundant. He and his wife moved the length of the country within three months of him heading into the next stage of his life. As we talked, he shared that twenty years ago, on a family vacation, he had decided that he was going to spend his later years close to three things that had presented themselves on this particular trip:

1. Family;
2. A top-class tennis club; and
3. The beach.

At just over fifty, and after close to thirty years with the same company, the move was made in consultation with all the family members living in the area. The first time I met the client, he said he had found a top-class tennis centre run by a former professional and was looking at purchasing a house within a few klicks of it. By the second session, he and his wife had found a townhouse 300 metres from the beach, two klicks from the tennis club, within twenty minutes' drive of family and, just to put a cherry on top, a few minutes' drive from a golf club, too. He couldn't have been happier transitioning into his new life. When he left me at the end of the second session, he said, 'Twenty years of planning and research has gone into this great result, you know. Now it's my time.'

That's a short and sweet success story. However, things don't always go so smoothly. I was talking to one of my associates while I was researching and putting this book together, and he shared with me the following tale. This has been echoed more than a few times by people I've met transitioning out of full-time work, and it's something to think about when deciding where you want to be located in the next stage of your life. Moving away from the place you've had to live due to work considerations is a no-brainer for a lot of people, and relocation can be a great source of fulfilment in the next stage of life, but it takes research and a lot of thought to get it right.

The couple my associate told me about had had the vision of moving to the coast for many years. Each time they had visited the coast, they'd been greeted with open arms by the members of the family who were living there. Some of the couple's most memorable times were spent near the beach. Most of the time, their visits coincided with school holidays, Christmas and Easter. Happy times when they were surrounded by people.

When the time came, they made the move. They sold their family house of many, many years, left their close friends, and downsized into an adequate home not too far from family members and acquaintances. However, this was done without in-depth consultation or conversation with the family members involved.

After the initial excitement of the move and spending some time with the family and grandkids, the couple began to feel more and more isolated. They found their family was involved in a lot of activities and life was planned outside of just seeing Grandpa and Grandma. They were used as babysitters when it was convenient for the parents to have a night off, and on maybe one in five or six weekends the couple spent quality time with the family they'd moved to be close to. At the same time, the couple found it hard to break into any social circles and found themselves frequently travelling to see their friends back in their home town.

To cut a long story short, before too long, they made the decision to move back to their home town. They were back near to their friends and social groups, but in a smaller townhouse in a location they had to settle for (because their moving costs were so large) rather than a place to really love and call home. Back where they began, though surrounded by friends their own age, they were in a state of regret and frustration and had blown a lot of money in the process.

How could they have avoided this?

Identifying where a person and their spouse wishes to live requires going through a series of realistic questions in order to ensure that the move is made for the right reasons. There are a lot of factors that need to be taken into consideration, and the vision has to be assessed against the reality of the move.

MAKING THE RIGHT MOVE

A move to the wrong location can be both costly and damaging to relationships.

The key here is to be clear on where you want to be and the reasons behind it. Then it is important to share your plans with anyone who may be affected by the relocation. It sounds simple enough to do; however, the process of getting to an end decision may involve asking some deeper and tougher questions, of yourself, your partner and other key players, than you might think.

Questions could include:

*   What are your motivations for the move?

    Often, we need to check in with our motivations for moving location. What is the real reason? Being closer to family to see the grandkids grow up and be part of their lives while you are still active and able? A sense of obligation? Because you have the time to dedicate to the move? You heard it was a great place to live from a friend of a friend? The key here is to be very clear on your motivations and take into consideration other people who may be affected by the move.

- What assumptions are you making about the move?

This question is all about considering your conscious and unconscious assumptions – and questioning others to check whether your assumptions are correct. Are you assuming that you'll get together with family every week for Sunday lunch? Do you expect to see family every day? Do you assume that they'll cook for you more often than not? Do you assume the climate will be better? That you'll meet other people your age and make friends easily? That your old friends will certainly come and visit regularly?

- What are the facts about the move?

This question is all about due diligence and taking the emotion out of the move. Really investigate the facts, truths and realities of making such a move and the effect it will have on all areas of your life. What expectations will others have if you do move? Will they expect to use you as an impromptu babysitter? What are the demographics of the area you're considering – will there actually be a large, active community of people you'll likely want to socialise with? Does the place have the facilities you're likely to need in the next stage of your life?

- What is the cost of living where you are headed?

  Finances simply have to be considered here. This takes time and research before making a decision. More and more people moving into the next stage are considering living overseas, where the lifestyle is perceived as either trouble free, luxurious or better value for money, etc. But even a move down the road may, in reality, increase your cost of living. And have you factored in flying back to visit friends and family? Be aware of the 'money illusion', especially when it comes to an international move.

- Whom do you need to have conversations with?

  Consider everyone who may be affected by the move, both in your current location and the location you're considering moving to. Talk to your partner/significant other, family members, friends, health practitioner(s), potential modified work life colleagues and bosses, club members for various activities you are involved in, and alumni from work/university/school.

What we are trying to avoid here is what I call 'Rose-coloured Glasses Syndrome'. In the midst of a major change in your life, you need to be very clear on your expectations versus the reality of a relocation.

Had our couple in the earlier story spent more time asking the right questions and involved the family members who were going to be affected, then there may well have been a different long-term outcome, without the loss of a few disappointing years.

I think it is important to acknowledge that in the course of moving into the next stage of your life, you will make a mistake or two; we are human, after all. However, when it comes to location, it is worth taking both the time and the effort to flesh out the issues.

In some cases, you may need to set up a good old-fashioned pros and cons matrix in order to unpack your head and get the things that are important to you onto paper.

Below is an example of a moving evaluation matrix. I used to do something similar with my career transition clients when they were evaluating options and needed just a little more than the overly simple pros and cons list. When my dad made his move to a location near a golf course, we used a similar matrix to make it more realistic and easier to evaluate. Making a move is often a more emotional decision than a well-considered one, so it pays to dig a bit deeper.

Here is an example:

Move factors	Weight (100 pts total)	Factor rating (1-5 Scale)	Total points
Location	25	4	25 x 4 = 100
Family	20	4	20 x 4 = 80
Friends and Social Life	15	4	15 x 4 = 60
Neighbourhood	13	3	13 x 3 = 39
Work Opportunities	12	3	12 x 3 = 36
Access to Activities	10	3	10 x 3 = 30
Beach/Water/Shopping	5	2	5 x 2 = 10
TOTAL	**100 points**		**355 points**

Your move factors may be different, but hopefully you get the point. By putting down in the matrix the most important factors to you, and then rating those factors for different locations you consider, you can evaluate any potential move.

Other factors that some of my clients have taken into account before making a move are in alignment with the wealths covered in this book, including: wellbeing, enhancing relationships, lifestyle and practicality.

One of my clients disliked the busy-ness of constant city life, but his partner loved it. Over the years, she had developed a strong social and community network, which he knew she wouldn't want to leave. Guided by his love of the country and with the realisation that his body needed rest over the coming years, he came up with what I thought was a great idea. He purchased a small block of land (about 5ha) about forty-five minutes from his city flat, and on it built a modest two-bedroom house with all he needed to get away and pursue his love of nature and his desire for solitude when it came up. It was a solution that catered for both parties involved.

When looking at your location for both the short and long term, get very clear about what you want and include all the parties involved to achieve a win/win/win. Like any negotiation, it is not always comfortable, but making sure you communicate means you move towards an outcome all parties can live with.

DOWNSIZING

For many, it is not relocation that is the big decision, but the question: What does downsizing look like?

Over the past few years, the idea of downsizing has become a hotly discussed topic, right down to the birth of the tiny house movement. If you are one of the 'empty nester' generation who finishes full-time work and finds their family home too big for their practical use, then downsizing is an attractive option.

This shift in location and size can be exciting, but, at the same time, not an easy process. You have to let go of your attachment to a home that you may have been established in for many years. Having lived in it for so long, the accumulation of stuff can be considerable. For many, the downsizing process can be daunting because it involves letting go, selling, giving away and donating some much loved but unused things associated with happy memories.

Many of my clients have gone through this process. They have shared that the hardest part of downsizing was getting started. After a short time, though, they got into a rhythm that allowed them to make practical decisions on what would stay, what would go to charity and what would be sold online or in a weekend garage sale.

Some clients, after they completed the downsizing process, said they felt 'lighter'. They actually found the exercise cathartic and freeing as they let go of the past and looked forward to the future without so much stuff. One client summed up the process extremely well. He said to me, 'Steve, you know the one thing I have learnt out of this downsizing business? I've learnt the most important things I have at this time in my life are not things.'

One of my married retired friends shared with me a simple observation: 'When we downsized we made sure we found a home that was big enough to lose ourselves in if we needed to and small enough to find each other when we desired.'

Some of you may consider having multiple homes. Quite a few of my clients have planned to split their time between two or more locations. Typically, the downsizing process includes selling the family house and then purchasing two smaller homes. The most common combination I have witnessed is an apartment in the city of origin and then a 'place by the sea' or 'up north'.

Another approach is having one townhouse or apartment to use as a base and then purchasing a campervan, caravan, camping trailer, mobile home or houseboat. Many of my clients end up with an agile second home. They're known as Grey Nomads (aka going SKI-ing- Spending the Kids' Inheritance), joining an increasing number of people in the next stage of their lives experiencing different destinations around the country. Some use a mobile home to take short trips, while others decide to do a lap of the country. On a trip to the Margaret River wine region, my wife and I came across a couple in their mid-sixties who were on their fifth trip around Australia in their mobile home. They said that they experienced something new each time. They loved it and said that there were people that they had met on several occasions doing the same thing.

As an indication of just how popular joining the Grey Nomads is, the number of caravan and campervan registrations has increased by over forty per cent in the last decade. At the time of writing, there are over 600,000 caravans and campervans registered throughout Australia.

Although there are a lot of things to think about in terms of possible relocation as you move into the next stage of your life, considering all of the issues carefully will reduce the risk of Rose-coloured Glasses Syndrome.

Like a big business deal in your work life, location and downsizing shifts in the next stage of your life require due diligence. By considering all the aspects that have been covered in this chapter, you not only reduce the risk of things going wrong, you increase the chance of your life being filled with more joy, happiness and contentedness in the coming years. That is why I consider location a wealth beyond money. Get location right and it can enhance and influence the other wealths – your Self, your Wellbeing, your Relationships, your Lifestyle, your Legacy and, for many, your Spiritual Development.

4. Relationships

'We exist only in relation – to our friends,
our family and our life partners...
In many ways, we are our relationships.'

—DERRICK BELL

QUESTIONS TO CONSIDER IN THIS SECTION:

- **What relationships in your life are most important to you?**
- **What aspects of your current relationships are working well?**
- **In the next stage of your life, what relationships may need renegotiation?**
- **Who do you want to spend your time with moving forward?**
- **How can you invest time in yourself, your partner, your family, your friends and your social networks?**

Relationships are the ultimate wealth.

Put simply, great relationships equal a great life. And when I talk about relationships, I mean your relationship with yourself as well as your relationships with your partner, with your family, with your friends, with people that you meet on a regular basis, and with people that you have just met.

A recently published eighty-year, longitudinal study, undertaken as part of the Harvard Study of Adult Development, found one surprising outcome. Close relationships are what keep people happy throughout their lives and in later years.

These close positive relationships protect people from life's discontents, and help delay mental and physical decline. The study found that ongoing and close relationships are better predictors of happy lives than social class, intelligence or inherited genes.

As the research suggests, relationships have the power to enrich your life. But they also have the power to negatively influence you during your journey into the next stage of your life. Toxic relationships can send you emotionally broke.

As human beings, one of the most complex animals on the face of the planet, this idea that we have constructed – called relationships – is one that cannot be easily defined.

There are all manner of relationships that we could explore, and there are more levels to relationships than you can poke a stick at; however, for the intentions of this book, we will concentrate on the five key relationships that affect most people:

1. Relationship with self (considered earlier in the book);
2. Romantic relationships;
3. Family relationships;
4. Relationships with friends; and
5. Casual relationships.

In their workshop 'The Infinite Power of Your Relationships', The Mind Matters Insistitute sum up in a nutshell what Rex

Urwin calls 'Relating-ships'. Relationships are conducted on one of three levels:

1. An intimate level;
2. A sharing level; or
3. A ritualistic level.

Most of our interactions day to day occur on the ritualistic level and are rather superficial in the way they play out. As we get to know people and loved ones, we open up and the relationship moves to the sharing level. The intimate level is reached when the relationship is open and we're free to share deeply personal thoughts, beliefs, experiences and information. When you get relationships to the higher levels, the quality rises. The relationships on these levels enrich your life. It's where you get the most out of relationship experiences.

By being aware of the levels and conscious of what level you're on with different people, you can not only assess your relationships but also work on the ones you want to develop further, especially if you wish to move from ritualistic to sharing relationships. This is powerful moving forward into the next stage of your life, where you want to enjoy the great source of wealth and happiness your relationships can provide.

RENEGOTIATING RELATIONSHIPS

A client once opened a meeting with the comment, 'I have realised, Steve, that the space in the kitchen has got a lot smaller in the past few weeks.'

It's an observation that sums up a lot about what happens in a couple's relationship when they transition into the next stage of their lives.

Meanwhile, for people who are single, it is fair to say that the spaces in the home get a lot cleaner! Small things that were not noticed during the busy-ness of work life come to the forefront when you spend more time at home.

The transition into your next age is a time of reorientation, as we saw in Bridges' Model. It is also a time of renegotiation of relationships – with yourself (which we have explored), and also with your family, your friends, and social and community connections, both old and new.

It's important to explore the effect of this transition on our relationships.

When relationships need to be renegotiated and the process is not handled well, conflict and resentment can result, building into a lack of confidence, lack of control and, in extreme cases, anxiety, fear, anger, confusion and stress.

In a family context, people's common expectation is that they will spend a lot more time with their family members, particularly their sons and daughters. However, it's necessary to explore the reality of this perception, keeping in mind that each family member may already have their own family, still have their work life, and be entrenched in their own routines, etc.

The solution for dealing with these evolving relationships, whether established or new, is a cornerstone for life in the next age: Open Communication. I know it's easier said than done; however, there are some simple strategies which can help you prepare for these revolutions in and renegotiations of relationships. With some work, you can make it so that, in the coming months and years, you are not majoring in minors when it comes to enjoying the next stage of your life with others.

Transitioning into the next stage of your life as a successful man is a bit like moving into a new role in your career – you have accepted the offer and now you have to plan your first ninety to a hundred days. There are many roles where there is a requirement to produce this plan early. In the context of maintaining, enriching and evolving relationships in the next stage of your life, it is definitely worth doing so.

Below is a suggested framework you can use to have a conversation with your life partner, family members and close friends in order to renegotiate, reinvent or evolve your relationships (if required) as you move into the next stage of your life.

This framework has an 80/20 foundation. In other words, the process is eighty per cent preparation and twenty per cent presentation.

Firstly, it's important to note that the success of the process depends on a few things:

1. An agreed pre-frame – i.e. an understanding such as: 'We are doing this because things are going to change or have changed. By doing this, we will have a stronger, more enduring and richer relationship.'

2. Having the end outcome in mind – i.e. Win/Win/Win: 'This is going to be a Win for me, a Win for you and a Win for both of us.'

Next, go through the process below:

1. **COME TO AN UNDERSTANDING OF WHAT YOU WOULD LIKE TO CREATE FOR EACH RELATIONSHIP**

   First, mentally shift from your business role into the next stage of your life. See this process of exploration, reorientation and renegotiation of roles and relationships as an investment in your future wellbeing and happiness, not a waste of time.

   Now, as you consider each relationship in your life, put down on paper the important aspects of your relationship, from most important to least important.

   Take your partner, for example. This process could include going through your values, which we explored earlier in the book, and assessing how they may affect your relationship moving forward. If, for example, one of your values is independence – something that has served you well in your working life – then you may want to write down what you perceive independence as meaning for you in the next stage of your life. How will that value be catered to going forward – in your relationship with your partner? How much 'Me' time do you need or desire in a day, week or month? What activities, development, learning or hobbies would like to do for yourself? What activities, development, learning or hobbies would you like to do together?

Ask yourself: What do you want to feel? What fun do you want to have and what does that look like for you both? Take into consideration the physical, mental and emotional demands you have of your partner – and that they have of you. This hurts! Why? Because we have to really think and spend time getting clear on what we have and what we want to create in our relationship moving forward.

Write down all the answers as if you're living in a perfect world and everything is hunky-dory first. You can always modify it later. Once you are clear on your ideal relationship and you have it down on paper, it's time to consider negotiation.

2. KNOW WHERE YOU ARE PREPARED TO COMPROMISE IN EACH RELATIONSHIP

Relationships are inevitably two-way streets. They involve exchanges of energy if they are going to stand the test of time. When you are spending between forty and sixty hours engaged in work, relationships can often survive many years because the time spent together is limited. When you move into the next stage of your life, you will naturally have more time to spend with people. Knowing what you want and where you can compromise are important starting points for handling the changing nature of your relationships in a proactive way.

In his article 'The Art of Microcompromise: How to survive compromises all relationships require', Alex Lickerman, MD points out that men can often be constrained by the 'Good Guy contract' and, as a result, may surrender their 'microneeds' over time. This causes resentment and can lead to a sudden explosion of emotion that a close partner may be totally shocked by. They are even more shocked to find that they have contributed to it in some way, shape or form. Dr Lickerman goes on to suggest three strategies to manage the 'microcompromises' that exist in all close relationships:

1. Recognise that by choosing to be in an intimate or sharing relationship that we pay a price, and that price is a constraint on our perceived 'total freedom' (to do what we want, when we want) so to speak.

2. Remember that you **chose** to be in the close and sharing relationship. So when you feel frustration building, remember that it is a result of your decisions. This can give you perspective on the situation.

3. Choose to see the microcompromises as a gift to your partner rather than as something you 'must' do. Dr Lickerman's observation of a successful intimate or sharing relationship is based on the recognition that microcompromises are gifts that are exchanged rather than demands that need to be met. If both partners are on the same page then when large compromises need to be made, it is less likely that resentment will play a major role in the process, as clear, empathetic and compassionate conversations occur that arrive at the best decision for both partners.

Here's a simple example: In a perfect world, I would rise at 6.00am and have a shower and shave at 6.15am. To me, that would be perfect to get the day off to a good start in the next stage of my life. However, in my work life, I am up at 5.30am to have full run of the bathroom. My partner is used to having the bathroom between 6 and 6.15am when I'm finished. So if I change to my ideal when I move into the next stage of my life, this may impact on my partner's routine. This sounds small; however, as the kitchen comment above suggests, without meaningful conversation and discussion on what is going to work moving forward, this small change in routine could escalate and undermine the relationship.

Humans are creatures of habit. So know what you want but also where you are prepared to negotiate.

3. ESTABLISH WHAT IS GOING RIGHT IN YOUR DIFFERENT RELATIONSHIPS

It's important to accentuate the positives. Part of the eighty per cent preparation for this process is about reflecting and really considering what is going well in the relationships you truly value as they are in the present.

Successful relationships that endure changes often do so because there is an ongoing recognition of what is going right in them. In other words, the focus is on the positive aspects most of the time. These are the primary focus. As a result, if an aspect changes and something impinges on a relationship, open, honest and frank conversations can be had that enhance and enrich the relationship rather than damage and denigrate it.

Accentuating what is going right in a relationship at the start of a conversation can be a good way to remind everyone of the value of the relationship before entering into the more difficult parts of the conversation.

4. DEVELOP QUESTIONS THAT ALLOW OPEN COMMUNICATION

How and what questions are a good starting point. Ensure that your questions are phrased in a way that moves towards something positive rather than avoiding the real issues.

Questions that open up possibility may be phrased as follows:

- What flexibility is there in...?
- How can we make... work more smoothly?
- What you think about...?
- How would you feel about...?
- Something that is important to me is... How about... as a way forward?
- How would you like to...?
- What is your preference for...?

If we stick with the example above regarding bathroom times, then some of the questions that might be developed to have a win/win/win result may go along the lines of the following:

One of the things that is important to me is morning routine in the next stage of our lives. My preference is to be showering at about 6.15am moving forward; however, I know that has been your routine for many years and I want to respect that. What flexibility might you have in your morning routine moving forward so I am not in your way?

And so the conversation begins.

5. MANAGE EXPECTATIONS AND SHARE THE AIM OF WIN/WIN/WIN OUTCOMES

If necessary, send a short email or letter so that all parties in the relationship are clear on the understandings and how things are moving forward as a result of your conversations.

This is about being clear and transparent so that there are no misunderstandings in the process. Get all parties in the conversations to convey in writing what they believe the outcomes/understandings have been.

This is worthwhile because, although we all live on the same planet, each one of us experiences the world around us (what we hear, what we see, what we understand) in a truly unique way. By getting the outcome according to each party on paper, any grey areas can be smoothed out easily.

Here's an example that some of you will be able to relate to if you have an interest in or passion for sport.

One of your negotiation points may have been the amount of football, rugby league, rugby union, soccer and/or AFL you might want to experience in the one or two months of finals footy that is available. After the conversation that you have had in the above process, you might acknowledge in writing that during the whole season you are willing to microcompromise and watch one match (split screen, of course) each weekend, and be available for other social activities on the rest of the weekend; however, you wish to be clear that the last two weekends of the season are totally reserved for indulging your passion of football in all its forms.

6. MAINTAIN A POSITIVE APPROACH TO THIS PROCESS

Note the short, medium and long-term benefits that will result from the changes in your close relationships moving forward.

Following the process means that you can remain in a grounded space as you have the required conversations. Doing so means that once these conversations have occurred, they can be revisited again as necessary as relationships evolve.

One of the short-term advantages is clarity, whether around the roles that you will play (house husband, grandfather, cook), the activities that you will do, or the expectations you have of your relationship with your intimate partner and others.

Some of your agreements/negotiated outcomes will probably only need to be covered and discussed once for clarity. Other aspects may have to be revisited time and time again over the coming years.

This is a chance to clear the slate and reinvent, renegotiate and/or enhance certain aspects of your relationships.

In the medium term, an understanding of each relationship can result in much less stress. Relationships run a lot smoother as new routines and activities are established and then become 'matter of course' parts of life.

In the long term, as the Harvard study revealed, by going through this process, happiness can be increased and sustained. Strong relationships can lead to ongoing healthy behaviours and a greater sense of purpose.

This process is valuable but not always comfortable. However, by going through it, you save yourself the pain of having to deal with these areas retrospectively when emotions are high (and intelligence can be rather low), when you might say or do something you later regret.

Negotiating outcomes early and often with all involved will ultimately lead to a productive outcome – one where each party knows what is going on.

Just coming to the awareness of the kitchen getting smaller, like my client at the beginning of the chapter, is a great first step towards dealing with the changing nature of relationships which occurs as you transition into the next stage of your life. That awareness can lead to acknowledging the change and then a cool, calm and collected discussion about the solution. This is opposed to a stand-up argument that might happen later down the line sparked by a totally unrelated incident or, worse, continuing to avoid the changing nature of the relationship altogether, resulting in greater consequences down the track.

With forty-three per cent of retirees reporting that the transition into the next stage of their lives was a challenge, it is worth the investment of time, energy and relationship building to address this part of your life well from the start. This will stop you having fights over minor things, having resentment build over personal space and being miffed by others' non-attention.

By working with people through relationship issues now, you will be in a much more positive position to discuss openly any issues that arise later than if they are left to simmer under the surface. This is good investment of your time as you transition into the next stage of your life.

Ultimately, your relationship with yourself and your relationships with intimate partners, family, friends and social contacts come down to trust and respect. With trust and respect present, you can access the wealth that is the reward of positive relationships.

5. Lifestyle and Modified Work Life

'Lifestyle is the art of finding ways to live uniquely.'

— JIM ROHN

QUESTIONS TO CONSIDER IN THIS PART OF THE BOOK:

- **What do you want for yourself?**
- **What do you have to offer?**
- **What do you want to do with your time?**

Recently, on an executive business course, I met a quietly spoken gentlemen with no sense of fashion at all. He was single, retired and, as it turned out, destined to be my roommate for the duration of the course. It wasn't until later that I learnt that this silent and socially awkward man was not only very wealthy, but very smart. He also had one of the most defined ideas of preferred lifestyle that I had come across in my time working with people transitioning from full-time work into the next stage of their lives.

Over a beer and a few rum and cokes, he shared with me that he loved maths and preferred nature on all levels to the company of human beings. As a result, when he left his final role, he bought a plot of land in the middle of nowhere. It was close enough to town to get what he needed when he needed it but far enough away to enjoy the silence of nature.

Three nights a week, he would be up at 2.00 am in the morning to trade the US stock market. His eyes lit up as he told me that he liked nothing better than sitting with a warm coffee on his wrap-around balcony, frantically trading numbers at the speed of light, yet aware of the relative stillness of nature around him, all under a crystal-clear, star-studded sky. When I asked him why he was on the course, he acknowledged that he believed in lifelong learning. He actually took at least three short courses a year in different life areas to keep him connected with people and to keep his mind stimulated.

My roommate knew the lifestyle he wanted and had taken action to make it a reality. He lived a life that marched with what he found important and true to his values, and embraced a life that he was content with. A smart man indeed.

What lifestyle do *you* want?

WHERE ARE YOU GOING?

There's an old saying: *If you don't know where you are going, how do you know when you get there?*

Men transitioning out of the full-time workforce need to have a clear idea of: who they are, what is important to them, what they prefer to do (and not do), what knowledge and skills they have (or would like to have), and how all of these aspects interconnect to provide opportunities for further work, self-development, activities, hobbies, social interaction and being part of communities in the next stage of their lives.

There are so many things to consider when it comes to lifestyle, whether you choose to focus on more recreational or professional pursuits. It's about what you will occupy yourself with in the stage of your life – a massive source of wealth.

Continuing self-development may include online or campus-based courses or seminars, writing, blogging, researching, and using and keeping up with technology.

Sport and active recreation may include walking, hiking, jogging, going to the gym, swimming, golf, tennis, bowls, as well as other sports and indoor and outdoor games.

Amusements and cultural interests can encompass a wide range of activities, like movies, theatre, TV, radio, music, playing an instrument, travel, vacations, museums, art shows, card games and board games.

Service activities include volunteer work and being active in service clubs and civic groups.

Social activities include phone calls, social networking through sites such as Twitter, Facebook and LinkedIn, in-home entertaining with small or large groups, family get-togethers and calling on friends.

Interests and hobbies could mean any variation of arts and crafts, collecting, DIY home improvement, gardening or mechanic or electric restoration, scrapbooking (not for every man), etc.

The key in determining your lifestyle is to work out what you want to do and then design your days, weeks, months and years ahead to incorporate all the aspects that make up a satisfying lifestyle according to you. Then, where necessary, you can negotiate and collaborate in order to create your desired lifestyle.

Some people want the beach lifestyle, some want the 'tree change' lifestyle, others want the warm weather lifestyle or the decadent lifestyle, luxury lifestyle, tranquil lifestyle, adventurous lifestyle, the mixed change and variety lifestyle... the list goes on.

There is no right or wrong way to create a lifestyle that you wish to enjoy. For many, it is something that evolves over time. The point here is to unpack your head and get your ideas down on paper.

When asked, people who are in the last few months of their lives and know the end is near rarely make reference to the material ownership of 'things'. What they do reflect on is experiences, memories and people. This is your chance to do it consciously.

Exercise: The Bucket List

Some people have a list of experiences that they wish to have in the coming years. This is often called the Bucket List. Build one for yourself, starting with way-out-there experiences (like space travel) and finishing with small, significant experiences (a weekend fishing with your son and grandson, for example).

Once you have the experience down, allocate a motivation rating to it, e.g. 10% = Little motivation; 100% = Absolutely motivated to make the experience a reality.

Experience (in order of most improbable to most probable)	Motivation Rating (%)

By unpacking your head and putting your experiences down on paper, you can start the planning process of making each experience happen, whether in the short, medium or long term.

Doing the above exercise helps because it activates a certain part of your brain called your Reticular Activating System (RAS for short). It sits at the base of your brain and acts as your internal radar.

The best way to illustrate how it works is the experience that many people have when buying a car. As soon as you make the decision to research or buy a certain make or model of car, have you ever noticed that you then start seeing that make or model everywhere you go? Before that point, you simply never consciously noticed the make and model. It was just another car passing by.

Now you've made the conscious decision to incorporate certain experiences into your lifestyle, you'll see the opportunities everywhere.

Spending time unpacking what lifestyle you want to create gives you power over time and space, to create what you want out of this stage of your life.

My course roommate knew exactly the lifestyle that he wanted and found a way to make it a reality. For most, it would not be the type of lifestyle that they would choose, but the point here is to live a lifestyle that suits *you*.

Though the focus of this book is 'beyond the money', it's obvious that your finances are going to set some boundaries in this space. You may need to spread out some of the experiences that you want to be part of your lifestyle. Not everyone will have the resources at hand to accomplish everything in the short term. This doesn't mean, however, that you shouldn't look to incorporate everything you want to achieve in the longer term.

We often overestimate what we should be doing in the short term and underestimate what we can achieve in the long run. We end up 'shoulding' ourselves as time goes by.

I have one client, Jimmy, who transitioned into the next stage of his life with about 100K less than he thought he needed in his superannuation fund. It became clear that he could not do all the lifestyle activities that he wanted to do each and every year. In particular, he couldn't afford a grand overseas trip every year. However, through our work together, he discovered that if he spread his wishes in that arena out to once every three years, for the next twenty-one years he could take those dream trips, both the ones he wished to take alone and the ones with his wife and family. Flexibility is the name of the game.

In his book *Living Rich*, Mark Ford suggests that we can all live rich; we just need to plan it a little. The most important message is that most of us can live very well, as well as do what we want to do – as long as we know what it is. When the money is sorted, life experiences, and enjoying them with appreciation, become the essence of living a meaningful life moving forward.

For some, what they genuinely want to do is continue working in some capacity, whether that means buying a business, becoming a consultant or corporate mentor, or volunteering for an organisation that they have a strong connection with.

The question is...

WHAT DO YOU WANT TO DO?

I have asked virtually every man who has walked through my door as a client in the past ten years this question: So what is it you want to do? I can literally count on four hands the number of men who have had a clear, specific answer, the exception being people who wanted the same job in the same industry.

When it comes to continued occupation or a modified work life as part of your lifestyle in the next stage of your life, it really revolves around two questions:

1. What knowledge and skills do you have?
2. What knowledge and skills do you wish to use, share or develop?

What Knowledge Do You Want to Use, Share or Develop?

Robert walked into my offices ready to retire and do part-time work. He loved gardening and said that he wanted to work in the gardening section of a major warehouse outlet ten minutes' drive from his house. Over several meetings, we devised both a short-term and long-term strategy for Robert in order to achieve his goal.

After thirty-five years using certain skills, he was very clear on what he did and didn't want moving forward. As it turned out, Robert took an interim part-time role that came via his network and continued to network and visit his desired workplace until an opportunity came up eighteen months later as part of the Christmas casual intake. He is now using the knowledge and skills he prefers to use.

Each person on the planet has what I call a knowledge and skills bank. You have a certain amount of knowledge about certain subjects that you are either interested in or that you have had to develop because of work or other activities. Your knowledge and skills bank consists of both practical and conceptual components.

When it comes to practical knowledge, I'm talking about information that is needed to achieve or conduct certain tasks, perform certain skills and participate in certain activities. In other words, specific information that can be applied through the development of skills via practice. This explicit knowledge is objective and rational knowledge that can be expressed in words, numbers or formulas.

A great example of gaining practical knowledge is learning how to swim with the assistance of an experienced coach or instructor and then being able to swim on your own. This example also includes experiential knowledge, required to attain the final outcome. In short, knowledge you can do physical activities with.

Other examples of practical knowledge include:

- Playing a piano
- Kicking a football
- Hammering a nail
- Playing a guitar
- Using an angle grinder
- Casting a fishing line
- Riding a bike
- Using a computer
- Hitting a golf ball
- Mixing music using a software package

When knowledge is based on understanding of concepts, principles, theories, models, classifications, imagination and ideas, it is called conceptual knowledge. It is knowing more than isolated facts and methods. It focuses on regrouping big understandings and corresponding relationships among them, i.e. linking relationships between separate pieces of information. Conceptual knowledge highlights connections between the concepts themselves. This knowledge has been acquired through purposeful and reflective learning.

Conceptual knowledge is also known as tacit knowledge. Subjective and experiential, this is knowledge that cannot easily be expressed in words, sentences, numbers or formulas; for example, technical skills involved in crafting works of art. It's when someone has know-how. In the performing arts, someone may be described as having the 'X' factor.

Examples of conceptual knowledge include:

- Leadership
- Philosophy
- Love
- Self-esteem
- Communication
- Creative and abstract thinking
- Problem-solving

Whatever knowledge you hold, it is your intellectual capital – you have it, you own it and you can choose to share it or develop it further.

One of the places to start is to brainstorm and unpack your head around what knowledge you have. It may seem like a simple process; however, this does take some thinking.

Exercise: My Knowledge

Allow yourself a good one to two hours to complete this task.

As discussed, knowledge comes in the different forms above. For example, you may have practical knowledge of sales processes, marketing, carpentry, language, maths, fishing or photography. You may have conceptual knowledge of leadership, innovation, intuition, humour, emotional intelligence or aesthetics.

Below is a matrix that you can use to input your knowledge. Once you know what is in your knowledge bank, you can spend some time considering what knowledge you might wish to share and what knowledge you might like to develop.

Fill out the table below, or download it as a worksheet at www.stevemendl.com.

	Knowledge I have	Knowledge to share	Knowledge to develop
Practical Knowledge			

	Knowledge I have	Knowledge to share	Knowledge to develop
Conceptual Knowledge			

Like Robert, one thing has to be clear to you: your end goal around the knowledge that you want to use, share and develop.

In 1597, Sir Francis Bacon proclaimed, 'Knowledge is power.' Now you can choose the knowledge – the power and energy – you wish to share and the knowledge you wish to develop in the coming years.

Patience is key when it comes to gaining and then applying new knowledge. But it is always okay to try something and not like it. At the very least, you won't die wondering whether you might have found it a source of wealth.

Patience is also the key when sharing knowledge – and power – with others. It may come easily to you because you have unconscious competence, but it may take longer for others to understand.

Your knowledge may be closely related to your skill areas. There is a cybernetic connection between your motivated skills and the knowledge you may wish to share and develop. This also ties in with your experience, past present and future.

What Skills Do You Want to Use, Share or Develop?

A gent came into my client rooms who was in the process of moving into the next stage of his life. I asked him one question: 'Is there anything that you might have done that you never followed through with?' His answer was short and sweet. 'Use my electrician skills, my original trade, and share those skills with others.'

Having identified the possibilities and opportunities within the client's travel tolerance, within two weeks, he was working twenty hours a week helping a major retailer set up the electrical section of a new store. First he was coordinating the set up of the section, and when that was done he would be a casual employee at the coalface, using the electrical tools in the course of customer service.

I call the skills you want to use your MI Skills: Your Motivated and Inspirational Skills. You enjoy using them, derive satisfaction from them and take pleasure from sharing them with other people.

It is important to distinguish those skills you are good at, but which, if given a choice, you would prefer not to use on a regular basis. Often, a person will be given a particular job or role to do because of some random event (a colleague is sick or you have to cover someone on holidays, etc.), and then because they do it well, they are then given more and more of the same work. Before they know it, they have a career in a role they fell into.

So, at this point, the questions really are: What skills do you like using? And what skills do you have little or no skill in but want to develop? The Motivated Skills exercise gives you that focus.

Exercise: Motivated Skills

Next to each of the skills below, make two decisions:

1. Whether you enjoy using the skill or not with the following classifications:

   - Enjoy Using   (EU)
   - Like Using   (LU)
   - Prefer Not to Use   (PNU)
   - Dislike Using   (DU)

2. Your proficiency in the skill:

   - Expert   (ES)
   - Competent   (CS)
   - Minimal   (MS)
   - No Skill   (NS)

- **Accounting:** The systematic process of keeping financial accounts.

- **Advising:** Offer or recommend the best course of action for someone or a group.

- **Analysing**: Figure out problems logically.

- **Aquaculture:** The rearing of aquatic animals or the cultivation of aquatic plants for food.

- **Auctioneering:** Conduct auctions by accepting bids and declaring goods sold.

- **Budgeting**: Economise, save, stretch money or other resources.

- **Carpentry:** Construct, maintain or restore buildings, fittings or furnishings.

- **Classifying**: Group, categorise and systemise data, people or things.

- **Creating music**: Write and arrange music.

- **Counselling others**: Facilitate insight and personal growth, guide, advise and coach students, employees or clients.

- **Calculating numbers and statistics**: Tally, count, compute quantities.

- **Dancing**: All types of dancing, from ballroom to Latin and from line dancing to hip-hop.

- **Deal with feelings**: Listen, accept, empathise, express sensitivity, defuse anger, remain calm, inject humour, appreciate.

- **Designing**: Create new or innovative practices, programs, products or environments.

- **Editing, proofreading**: Check written material for proper usage and stylistic flair, make improvements.

- **Entertaining**: Poetry, comedy, public speaking, delivering messages to an audience.

- **Evaluating**: Assess, review, critique feasibility or quality.

- **Expediting**: Speed up production or services, trouble-shoot problems, streamline procedures.

- **Fishing**: Deep sea, angling, rock, river, lake, fly fishing, etc.

- **Food preparation**: Wash, cut, blend, bake and arrange for nutrition, taste and aesthetics.

- **Genealogy**: Research the line of descent traced continuously from an ancestor or family.

- **Generating ideas**: Reflect upon, conceive of, dream up, brainstorm ideas.

- **Gardening**: Tending and cultivating plants, lawns and landscape for visual appeal.

- **Hosting**: Make welcome, put at ease, provide comfort and pleasure, serve visitors, guests or customers.

- **Implementing**: Provide detailed follow-through of policies and plans.

- **Initiate change**: Exert influence on changing the status quo, exercise leadership in bringing about new directions.

- **Interview for information**: Draw out subjects through incisive questioning.

- **Liaising**: Represent others, serve as a conduit between individuals and/or groups.

- **Learning**: The acquisition of knowledge or skills through study, experience or being mentored.

- **Maintaining records**: Keep accurate and up-to-date records, log, record, itemise, collate, tabulate data.

- **Making arrangements**: Coordinate events, handle logistics.

- **Making decisions**: Make major, complex or frequent decisions.

- **Managing projects**: Initiating, planning, implementing and completing the work of a team or individual towards a specific goal or outcome.

- **Meditate**: Spend time focusing on one's mind for spiritual purposes or for relaxation.

- **Monitoring**: Keep track of the movement of dates, people or things.

- **Motivating people**: Recruit involvement, mobilise energy, stimulate peak performance.

- **Negotiating**: Bargain for rights or advantages.

- **Observing**: Study, scrutinise, examine data, people or things scientifically.

- **Perceiving intuitively**: Sense, show insight and foresight.

- **Performing**: Act, dance, sing, public speaking, stand-up comedy.

- **Planning, organising**: Define goals and objectives, schedule and develop projects or programs.

- **Planting**: Grow food, flowers, trees or lawns, prepare soil, plant, water, fertilise, weed, harvest, trim, prune, mow.

- **Photography**: Capture life and landscapes through a lens.

- **Physical coordination and agility**: Walk, run, climb, scale, jump, balance, aim, throw, catch or hit.

- **Portraying images**: Paint, sketch, draw, illustrate.

- **Producing crafts**: Shape, build, attach, etch or carve ornamental gifts or display items.

- **Problem-solving**: Find solutions to challenging issues.

- **Programming**: Programming and coding on computers.

- **Reading**: Read written resources for both information and pleasure.

- **Researching**: Research resources efficiently and exhaustively for relevant information.

- **Restoration**: The process of returning something to a former condition.

- **Selling**: Promote a person, company, goods or services, convince of merits, raise money.

- **Stage shows**: Produce theatrical, art, fashion or trade shows and other events for public performance or display.

- **Supervising activities**: Oversee, direct the work of others.

- **Synthesising**: Integrate ideas and information, combine diverse elements into a coherent whole.

- **Teaching, coaching, training**: Inform, explain, give instructions to students, employees or customers.

- **Tending animals**: Feed, shelter, breed, train or show domestic pets or farm animals.

- **Testing**: Assess proficiency, quality or validity, check and double-check.

- **Treating, nursing**: Heal, care for patients or clients.

- **Transport**: Drive, carry or haul in order to reach a destination.

- **Travel blogging**: Blogging while travelling the country or world.

- **Using mechanical abilities**: Assemble, tune, repair or operate engines or other machinery.

- **Vlogging**: Run a YouTube channel on a subject you are passionate about.
- **Videography**: Create videos for family and a wider audience.
- **Visualising**: Imagine possibilities, see in mind's eye.
- **Writing**: Compose reports, letters, articles, ads, stories or educational materials.

Below, list your top ten enjoyable (EU) skills regardless of skill proficiency:

My Top 10 MI Skills are (in order):

Skill #1: _____

Skill #2: _____

Skill #3: _____

Skill #4: _____

Skill #5: _____

Skill #6: _____

Skill #7: _____

Skill #8: _____

Skill #9: _____

Skill #10: _____

These skills can provide you with focus as you decide on the activities that you might want to be involved in as you move forward, both now and in the future. When it comes to your PNUs and DUs, look to delegate these when they are presented to you. Don't volunteer for them, regardless of your skill level. They represent your burnout zone and you will resent having to use the skills for any prolonged period of time.

Learn to say 'no' and negotiate in order to use the skills you enjoy and take part in the activities you want to be involved, in rather than being attracted to areas you're just good at.

GOING TO WORK: AN ENCORE CAREER

Work can take many forms. From career shifting into a new part-time role in a totally different industry through to volunteering a few hours a week for a cause that you have a connection with, I have taken many clients through a multitude of options with the aim of developing a customised work plan as part of the bigger transition picture.

The opportunity here is to combine some of the elements that we have covered and bring them together to come up with work that you want to do, in an industry you want to work in and in a manner that you dictate. This is something you do consciously, not just on automatic pilot and to satisfy other people's requests.

Daniel was a client who came into my office very clear about implementing a staged move into the next part of his life.

Having worked hard for over thirty-five years, he wasn't ready for retirement; however, he did want to do less work and spend more time with his wife and the newly arrived grandkids.

I asked what this looked like for him and he pulled up a spreadsheet on his laptop. In front of me were the numbers: 1,000, 500, 250 and 0. I asked him to tell me more. Daniel said, 'These are the number of hours per year I want to work in the coming decade. I want to start the reduction of my paid work life by working 1,000 hours per year, either twenty hours per week or six months of work at full-time load. Either way, I want to have a lot more time to myself and my family.' When I commented that what he had down was very specific, his reply was, 'I'm a very specific kinda guy.' That's an engineer for you!

Now, most people are not that specific when they first see me. They're not sure how they want engagement with an occupation to evolve in the next stage of their life. However, Daniel's story highlights an important point: It's good to have a plan.

There are several ways that you can weave work into the next stage of your life. Time and time again, I have heard the phrase: 'But I'm not ready to retire,' from my clients.

It's important to embrace the idea that the next phase of your life is not retirement from life. It is only the next stage of your life. If you have a sharp mind, a healthy body and willingness to take action, then there are many opportunities to make work an ongoing part of it all moving forward.

There are so many different types of work to choose from:

- Part-time or casual work for a company or organisation
- Consulting to organisations in your areas of your expertise
- Volunteering for organisations
- Starting or purchasing a business

Choose which type of work will best fit in with your desires for your lifestyle.

I have had clients do a mixture of casual work and volunteering. I have had clients who have started consulting because people have approached them for their expertise. I have had clients decide to fully devote their time to a particular cause or organisation on a volunteer basis. And I have had a few clients who have decided they never want to work in any shape or form for the rest of their lives. It would be fair to say, though, that the latter have been few and far between.

Most men not only want to do *something* in the next stage of their lives, but actively want to share their experience, knowledge and skills with other people. For many, this makes for a meaningful life.

You don't have to be as anal as Daniel when considering what working looks like for you in the coming years. However, it is worth considering what you might want to do and what industry you'd like to work in. Now you've assessed not only the knowledge and skills you have but those you want to develop, you can be as specific as the clients I've mentioned or as vague as knowing you'd just like to do something that involves contact with people. It is up to you. You are in control of what you want to do and not do.

For many successful men, one of the reasons they maintain a work life is either out of habit or because they want to keep their minds and bodies stimulated in the coming years. I once worked with a gentleman who used to be the general manager of a multi-national company. In his next age, he purposefully chose to work in the suits department of a well-known clothing store. Why? He knew that he couldn't move as quickly as the guys in the socks and jocks department, and he enjoyed developing a relationship with his customers, now and into the future. When a customer buys a suit, it is on purpose – often for a big event. He saw this as an opportunity to make the experience special. He worked in the same department for over ten years and finally left at seventy-eight years of age. Not bad, hey?

Never underestimate the wealth to be found in continuing to contribute in the roles that you have available to you moving forward. You can really make a difference. This leads beautifully onto the next chapter on legacy.

6. Legacy

'You are happiest
while you are making the greatest contribution.'

— JOHN F KENNEDY

QUESTIONS TO CONSIDER IN THIS PART OF THE BOOK:
- **What do you want to contribute?**
- **What do you want people to remember you for?**
- **What legacy will you leave behind?**

I want to open this chapter with a story, adapted from *The Star Thrower* by Loren Eiseley.

Once upon a time, there was an old man who used to go to the ocean to do his writing. He had a habit of walking on the beach every morning before he began his work. Early one morning, he was walking along the shore after a big storm had passed and found the vast beach littered with starfish as far as the eye could see, stretching in both directions.

Off in the distance, the old man noticed a small boy approaching. As the boy walked, he paused every so often and as he grew closer, the man could see that he was occasionally bending down to pick up an object and throw it into the sea. The boy came closer still and the man called out, 'Good morning! May I ask what it is that you are doing?'

The young boy paused, looked up and replied, 'Throwing starfish into the ocean. The tide has washed them up onto the beach and they can't return to the sea by themselves. When the sun gets high, they will die, unless I throw them back into the water.'

The old man replied, 'But there must be tens of thousands of starfish on this beach. I'm afraid you won't really be able to make much of a difference.'

The boy bent down, picked up yet another starfish and threw it as far as he could into the ocean. Then he turned, smiled and said, 'It made a difference to that one!'

LEAVING A LEGACY

This wealth area is about making a contribution and leaving a legacy.

There are many ways to leave a legacy and no right or wrong way to go about it.

I'll always remember my client Dave coming into my office for a session. He was in a hurry. 'Okay,' he said, 'let's get this over and done with. I have work to do.' As it turned out, Dave was catching a plane the next day to Cambodia, where he was going to project-manage the drilling of a series of bores and the building of several water stations. He was doing this to provide the local villagers with much-needed fresh water close to where they were located, instead of having to walk half a day in order to collect what we in the western world would take for granted out of a tap in our home.

About a month later, Dave and I caught up again and looked at his bigger plan for the next stage of his life. He revealed that he would be heading over to Cambodia several times over the coming years to monitor the progress. He wanted to maintain what he termed his 'little but significant contribution and legacy for the future'. It may have been small for Dave, but I would think his contribution has had and will continue to have a massive impact on the people of the villages that he and his team have been assisting.

Every successful man has the opportunity to take the time to really think about what they want to contribute and leave to the world, the city, the local neighbourhood or his household as a legacy.

So, the question becomes: What is going to be your legacy and contribution?

PHILANTHROPY

One way to contribute and leave a lasting legacy is through philanthropy, including volunteering and gifting. This can be done on a local, national or international scale.

There are several ways to conduct philanthropy:

SOCIAL ENTREPRENEURSHIP

Over the past several years, organisations and companies have been created to support something called social entrepreneurship – the use of entrepreneurial principles in taking on and aiming to improve society's challenges. Good social entrepreneurship programs and organisations will often offer a combination of financial and network support for chosen areas of focus.

CORPORATE PHILANTHROPY

This involves making a contribution through a company that has an awareness of their responsibilities in the wider community over and above making corporate profits. One of the best examples of this is the SONY Foundation, which looks to contribute to the advancement of the community by assisting youth and fostering their talents. Another example close to my heart is CanTeen – an organisation that supports teenagers living with cancer.

GRANT-BASED OR SCHOLARSHIP PHILANTHROPY

One option is to contribute money and/or time to an organisation that receives submissions for funding for particular projects, activities or organisations based on predetermined criteria or their potential impact on the target community.

ONE-OFF MONETARY GIFTS

As the name suggests, this is about making a one-off donation to an organisation that has a vision that resonates with you. Your money can assist in the realisation of a service or product that improves the lives of people and improves a societal situation, helping achieve a vision you believe in.

Venture philanthropy or Social Investment has emerged over the past few years with the realisation that there is a growing need for support and flexible funding for worthy causes and projects. This type of philanthropy utilises a diverse range of financing mechanisms, including grants, loans, micro-financing, equity and hybrid financing, which are tailored for the requirements of the target organisation.

There are so many options.

You might make a donation or you might undertake a series of short projects over a period of time or make a twenty-year commitment to a community group, charity or cause that you are passionate about or have a strong connection to.

My father was passionate about the vision, mission and activities of Lions Clubs International. When he moved into the next stage of his life, he stepped up his contribution in the club. Originally, it was on a local level, becoming the local club President, but later he went on to be a District Vice President and then District Governor. Some of his initiatives still exist as ongoing projects for the organisation. As a person who received an organ donation (kidney), he was passionate about the country-wide organ donation program. He was one of the early pioneers and advocates of a program that is really only gaining traction now as more people are affected by the issue. He never forgot, mentioned often, and was always very grateful to the young man who had completed the donor card. That person's legacy was to give my dad another ten good years leading a life of increased quality. My understanding is that five other people benefited from the young man's legacy. A legacy that lives on in others.

If you're already making a contribution, then the question is how you can magnify or add to the contribution in a way that can leave a lasting legacy.

For some people, it is a scholarship in their name. For others, it is service on a committee or board. Some set up a foundation for a target group of people. Others simply donate funds to their chosen organisation – one that makes a difference in people's lives.

One of my clients was a returned serviceman. He had a high-standing profile within the RSL sub-branch he was involved with. He noticed that a lot of the younger returned services personnel suffered from post-traumatic stress disorder and he wanted to assist them, given that he had suffered from the same mental health issues. He booked himself into a counselling course and by the time we had finished our program, he was well on the way to making a difference to others going through a similar experience. He was thriving because of it. What a legacy – showing empathy for his fellow humans and being a source of support for those who needed him.

Here I want to quote Bessie Anderson Stanley (whose words are sometimes attributed to Ralph Waldo Emerson):

'To laugh often and much;

to win the respect of intelligent people and the affection of children;

to earn the appreciation of honest critics and endure the betrayal of false friends;

to appreciate beauty;

to find the best in others;

to leave the world a bit better, whether by a healthy child, a garden patch or a redeemed social condition;

to know that even one life has breathed easier because you have lived.

This is to have succeeded.'

Ultimately, the measure of legacy is a subjective one, and it is a personal one. I just want to stress the untold wealth that lies in leaving something behind. There have been a number of studies done exploring the wishes and regrets of people in their last days. When questioned about what they would change in their lives, rarely would they have chosen to spend more time working. They would rather have contributed something – and known that more lives breathed easier and richer because they lived.

7. Spiritual Development

'The mind of a perfect man is like a mirror.
It grasps nothing. It expects nothing. It reflects but does not hold.
Therefore, the perfect man can act without effort.'

— CHUANG TZU

QUESTIONS TO CONSIDER IN THIS PART OF THE BOOK:

- **What will be returned to you?**
- **What do you focus on?**
- **What are you grateful for?**

The word 'spirituality' can put people off, but if you keep an open mind, there's a world of wealth to be discovered in this area. Spirituality isn't just about being seriously religious or a New Age hippy (though why not, if that attracts you?) – and it shouldn't be dismissed out of hand. While, for some, spirituality is found in religion, for others it is found in nature, meditation, self-contemplation or social and community life.

Spirituality is about the desire to be part of something bigger than yourself, and forming your purpose moving forward within the context of spirituality can be extremely powerful.

Jay had worked most of his forty-year career in the mines; however, he loved surfing. He was very up front with me about the fact that he was heading for the coast during our coaching program and told me that things were going to be pretty hectic, as he was moving with his wife to be near the sea.

I enquired further about the move and he was as clear as I have ever heard any of my clients be about why he was moving. 'Steve,' he said, 'I was brought up in the outback and there is something special about that, being in the middle of nowhere in the heat and the dust, being able to see all the stars at night. But for me, I have never felt so relaxed and calm as I do when I'm on the ocean. I get to think uninterrupted, even if I'm having a crap day's fishing or the surf's not real great.'

Although not formally spiritual, what Jay described is spiritual in essence.

In my world, spirituality can be summed up in the following words: 'To find beauty in all people, all nature and in even the tiniest of things is to appreciate the essence of life and all it has to offer and give.'

There are two concepts I want to take you through that can help you appreciate the wealth to be found in this area: the Law of Attraction and the practice of gratitude. Whether or not you already have your own spiritual creed, the next stage of life is a great opportunity to explore such ideas and beliefs further, finding meaning in this mysterious arena.

THE LAW OF ATTRACTION

This is a concept that has been around since the beginning of time.

When I was younger, every now and then I would have a day when my perception was that everything was going wrong. In short, I had got up on the wrong side of the bed and my focus was on all the bad things that happened that day. This was despite there being, on reflection, many good things that I could have focused on throughout the day, too.

As George Lucas's character Qui-Gon Jinn says in the first episode of *Star Wars*, 'Your focus is your reality.'

The Law of Attraction states that if you focus on bad things then more bad things will appear. If you focus on the good things, then you will experience more of the same.

The reality for many successful men is that they have had to keep a sharp focus on managing risk and anticipating problems, because it has been a large part of their responsibilities at work. But when preparing to leave employment, it is important to shift the focus from risk mode to positive mode.

Choose to be conscious of where you are operating from as you prepare to leave full-time employment.

The Law of Attraction states that like attracts like. If you operate from a place of positivity then, by and large, you will experience positive things. If you come from a place of negativity, then you are likely to attract more negative experiences.

So if you do find yourself confronted with fear, frustration, confusion and stress, it's important to somehow find a way to move as quickly as possible towards creativity – as demonstrated in Bridges' Transition Model, which we looked at in the first part of the book.

Knowing how powerful it can be, I can now move a lot more quickly from negative to positive, conscious and certain that I can spend less time in a negative frame.

Focusing on the negative aspects of life is rampant in our western society. Just look at the news – very little of it is positive. As a result, many people spend a lot of time thinking about what they don't want instead of what they do want.

Yet, the more you think about something, the more likely it is to be attracted to you. In her book *E-Squared: Nine Do-It-Yourself Energy Experiments That Prove Your Thoughts Create Your Reality,* Pam Grout offers the reader a series of exercises to test the Law of Attraction. The reverse vision exercise below works along the same lines. You might like to give it a go.

Exercise: Reverse Vision

This is a simple but powerful way to invoke the Law of Attraction. It involves putting yourself three, five or anywhere up to twenty years into the future and pretending that you are already there.

You then look back on what you have done and achieved in the allotted time, assuming that everything you ever wanted and planned has come through for you. You can do this with reference to each of the wealth areas covered in this book, adding your financial situation as well.

Now, put pen to paper or start typing away as if you were writing to an old friend about everything. I get my clients to start as follows:

Good morning (or evening)… I am so happy and grateful that…

Pen the rest of the letter.

This can be a very effective way of envisioning the future and it offers a great way to tap into the Law of Attraction since your focus is on everything that *has* gone right, rather than what *could* go wrong.

One of my long-term clients once completed a series of exercises with me, considered them for a few weeks and then promptly forgot about them. He shared with me three years later that he had found the exercises when moving house and had been pleasantly surprised to find that he had created and was doing about eighty per cent of what he had written down on a weekly, monthly and yearly basis.

When he reread his Perfect Day activity list (something we'll look at together in the third part of the book), he realised that he'd actually lived it in the most unexpected way.

He'd been on an overseas trip and all the diverse elements of his perfect day had come together: exercise, a leisurely breakfast, meditation, adventure, contribution, dinner with friends and music.

Setting intentions and focusing on what you want is beyond important. You attract what you focus on.

When you combine the Law of Attraction with gratitude, I have seen this change people's lives significantly for the better.

GRATITUDE

There were once two men, both seriously ill, who shared the same hospital room. One man got a bed next to the room's only window. The man was also allowed to sit up in his bed for an hour each afternoon to help him drain fluid from his lungs. The other man had to spend all his time lying flat on his back.

The two roommates quickly bonded and started talking for hours on end. They talked about their lives, their jobs, their children and wives. One day the man lying down expressed how much he envied the man near the window. From that day, the man near the window started describing all the things he could see outside.

The window overlooked a lovely park with a lake. Ducks played on the lake while children sailed their model boats. Young lovers walked arm in arm amidst flowers of every colour and a fine view of the city skyline could be seen in the distance. The man on the other bed began to live for those hours when he could hear and visualise the world outside the hospital room. One hour of every day would broaden his world and he was enlivened by all the activity and colour of the world outside.

One fine afternoon, the man by the window described a parade passing by. Although the other man could not hear the band, he could visualise it as the man by the window vividly described every detail.

Days and weeks passed.

One morning, a nurse arrived to examine the condition of the two patients. She found the lifeless body of the man by the window. The man had peacefully embraced his death in his sleep. The nurse sadly called the hospital attendants to take the body away.

The other man grieved the death of his roommate. As the days passed by, he particularly missed the way his roommate used to describe the view out of the window. In the hope of having a peek at the beautiful world outside, he asked if he could be moved. The nurse happily made the switch. As soon as he was comfortable in his new bed, the man slowly and painfully propped himself up to take his first look at the world outside. The nurse watched, delighted, as the man attempted to sit, having before only been able to lie on the bed. But as he strained to slowly turn to look out of the window beside him, he was stunned to see nothing but a blank wall outside the window.

The agitated man asked the nurse what could have made his roommate lie about the view. 'There is nothing to see from here. Where are all the wonderful things he saw? He described everything so vividly. Is this a new wall? Why did he give me such vivid details about things that didn't exist?'

The nurse shook her head and answered his question. 'Perhaps he just wanted to encourage you and make you happy. You see, your roommate was totally blind.'

It's all too easy to lose our perspective on things. We get caught up in what Anthony Robbins and others call 'majoring in minors'.

All too often, we compare ourselves with the Joneses and find ourselves getting discouraged about where we are, what we're looking for and where we are going. If things are headed south in this way, there's nothing more important than recognising what there is to be thankful for.

The results of the Village Project, conducted by the United Nations and others, are very helpful when it comes to finding your true north and regaining your sense of PERSPECTIVE in life. It was discovered that if the population of the world were reduced to a small town of 100 people, it would look something like this:

- There would be: 60 Asians, 11 Europeans, 14 Americans, including northern and southern Americans, and 15 Africans.
- 50 would be women, 50 men.

- 70 would have coloured skin, 30 would be Caucasian.

- 89 would be heterosexual, 11 homosexual.

- 1 person of the 100 would own 50% of the world's wealth and control 50% of its currency.

- 16 would be malnourished or starving.

- 70 would be undereducated.

- 50 would be underfed.

- 47 would have Internet.

- For each 1 to die, 2 would be born.

- 84 would live on less than $20 a day.

- About 4 or 5 would own a computer and only 2 out of the 100 would have access to higher education (i.e. a university degree).

- Out of the 100, more would have mobile phones than toothbrushes.

This morning, if you woke up healthy, then you're happier than the million people who will not survive the week.

If you have never suffered war, experienced the loneliness of a jail cell or the agony of torture or hunger, you're more fortunate than 500 million people on the face of the planet.

If you can enter a church, mosque, temple or other place of worship of your choosing without fear of jail or death, you're more fortunate than three billion out of the seven billion people on the face of the planet.

If there is food in your fridge, you have shoes and clothes, and you have a bed along with a roof over your head, the chances are that you are richer than seventy-five per cent of the people in the world.

If you have a bank account, money in your wallet and some coins in a money box, you belong to the eight per cent of people in the world who are considered well-to-do.

If you can read this book, you're absolutely blessed because you don't belong to the 800 million people around the world who cannot read.

So how are those apples? Perspective is a very powerful concept and allows us to see the world in a different light. This is particularly important in times of transition, when people can often lose sight of what is really important.

So many of my mentors and authors I have studied over the years , including Wallace D Wattles, Catherine Connelly, Rex Urwin and Anthony Robbins, have emphasised that the key to a great life – regardless of your 'station' in life – is to focus on and have gratitude for what you have.

When any man, no matter who they are or what they have done in their lives, awakens to the feeling of being grateful for who they are and what they have got, the world takes on an amazing transition in itself.

I was on a ship once, in the middle of possibly the clearest, bluest ocean I have ever seen, watching a pod of dolphins.

A close friend of mine standing beside me took a big breath and muttered the word 'magnificent'. And that moment truly was magnificent. It made the whole world seem magnificent, in every aspect. It was like all events, all aspects, all life had collapsed into one moment that was absolutely sensational. It was a feeling of magic that could not be mistaken, not often to be repeated.

Gratitude, in all its forms, increases the vibration of the human race from mediocre to vibrant. Knowing it, understanding it, living it and sharing it with as many as people as possible is the greatest change that any single human can make on the face of the planet.

One of my clients, Henry, came into my office having taken a voluntary redundancy from his employer. He was so grateful that, after thirty plus years of work, he had enough money to do what he wanted. And this included running a small but beautiful farm. He was grateful on every level that he could be a part of the farm. The team he got together, the work, the culture, the effort and the energy all came together to make his work more than worthwhile – it truly carried with it the feeling of making a difference in the world.

It is time to be grateful! So what can you be grateful for right now?

Here is a list to start your mind moving in the grateful space:

1. A healthy family.
2. A great home to live in. A roof over your head.
3. Netflix.
4. A healthy body.
5. A great group of friends.
6. The choice to do what you want.
7. A great partner in life.
8. High-speed Internet.
9. Your car of choice.
10. Nature around your house.
11. Someone to clean your home.
12. Living in a great part of the world.
13. Access to technology.

As you can see, the things you can be grateful for don't always have to be enormous – and can often be things you'd usually take for granted. It may well be as simple as the fact that you have two eyes and you are able to read this book rather effortlessly.

Below is your chance to fill out what you're grateful for. I call it your gratitude or fortunate list. Keep it simple or consider it more deeply – the list is up to you.

Exercise: Gratitude List

I am so happy and grateful to be one of the most fortunate humans on the face of the earth. I am grateful because…

1: _____

2: _____

3: _____

4: _____

5: _____

6: _____

7: _____

8: _____

9: _____

10: _____

11: _____

12: _____

13: _____

You now have a gratitude list, but don't leave it there! Daily or weekly or as often as you like, revisit your list. Refine and add to it over the coming days, months and years. Make gratitude a cornerstone of the next stage of your life.

From my experience of the world in the 21st century, there is no definitive right or wrong when it comes to your spirituality. It really is whatever you want it to be.

I have travelled much of this grand planet we live on over the years and what I have observed is that you can find the good, the bad, the ugly, the cool, the righteous and the pretend right across the world. Despite the differences, the sun still rises every day and there are good and bad deeds conducted day to day.

As I mentioned at the start of the chapter, spirituality is about the desire to be part of something bigger than yourself, and forming your purpose moving forward within the context of spirituality can be extremely powerful.

Now you've done all the hard work. You've covered the seven wealth areas of life beyond money: Self, Wellbeing, Location, Relationships, Lifestyle and Modified Work Life, Legacy and Spiritual Development. My hope is that it has been a good use of your time.

So what do we do next with all the exploration that has come before? In the final section, there are a series of frameworks that will allow you to develop your own plan as you transition into the next stage of your life.

Part 3:
Form a Plan

*'Our goals can only be reached through a vehicle of a plan, in which
we must fervently believe, upon which we must vigorously act.
There is no other route to success'*

— PABLO PICASSO

Part 3
Formal Plan

1. Expectations and Strategies

'We set goals not for what we GET, but for what we BECOME.'

— ANDREW MATTHEWS

Two of my long-time mentors, Rex Urwin and Catherine Connelly, are the founders of Mind Matters and NeuroCoding. The innovative, science-based methodology of NeuroCoding works through codes and neural pathways that we have all developed over the course of our lives. They include foundation codes, emotion codes, memory codes, attention, decision and planning codes, power codes, and movement, vision and language codes. Together the codes make us who we are, dictating what we believe is true, how we act and how we respond to our life and the events that take place within it.

Rex and Catherine continually teach that meaningful and successful lives are firstly imagined, then designed and finally lived.

What this means for you is that you first need to picture what you wish to be, do and have in alignment when it comes to the seven wealth areas in the future. In other words, create a vision of what you want. We did this in the future fitness and the reverse vision exercises earlier in the book.

In this section, we want to set expectations and the first expectation is that everything will go right or fall into place in order for the final vision to become true. Let the word 'but' go. At this initial stage, it is all about imagination... so let your imagination go wild and be free of all the objections. Some of you may feel that this is a bit fluffy and head-in-the-clouds, and in a sense you are correct. It is! However, engaging your imagination is only the first part of the process. As a wise old Japanese mentor of mine once said, 'Suspend your judgement,' and as another mentor reminded me, 'Trust the process.'

The second aspect of the process is to design a meaningful and successful life for yourself, incorporating what and who is important to you, and building this design based on your vision. This process is a lot more concrete and the frameworks provided in this part of the book will allow you to unpack your vision to make the experience you want to have a reality. It is your plan, your strategy, your blueprint, your roadmap, your pathway (whatever you want to call it) for a successful transition into the next stage of your life.

The third aspect of the process is to act and take steps towards what you have imagined and designed. As the saying goes, 'The journey of 1,000 miles starts with a single step.' I have adapted that adage for the 21st century: 'The journey of 1,000 miles starts with an airline ticket.' Your airline ticket is all the work you have done in the previous chapters in this book. The frameworks you're going to go through will now allow you to make your vision a reality.

Now we've explored the seven wealth areas, it's time to record a real plan or design for the next stage of your life. With awareness of the world of wealth out there to explore – beyond the money – you can now engage your imagination, set your expectations and design the perfect next age, whatever that means for you. You can then set down an action plan that will enable you to enjoy a smooth transition into this massively different part of your life. In this part of the book, you'll find strategies and exercises to help you on your way.

Exercise: A Vision of the Next Age

In this section, allow yourself to go nuts. As mentioned, this is the imagination part of the process, so do it free of judgement (we can always get practical later in the design process). Go into this part of the process with a 'blue-sky' attitude; don't hold back. Cover all of the seven wealth areas. For this exercise, you can also include finances to complete the vision:

1. Self
2. Wellbeing
3. Location
4. Relationships
5. Lifestyle and Modified Work Life
6. Legacy
7. Spiritual Development
8. Finances

This exercise is similar to the reverse vision exercise that you did earlier in the book. The difference in your vision is that you want to own it and create it in the present tense.

Remember, you are in control of the vision – what you include, what you leave out, the time line of the vision. It is up to you. By doing this, you are starting to NeuroCode your future.

Spending some time questioning your expectations and creating a vision of your next age will allow you to develop a truly informed plan which includes key indicators, milestones and goals.

Reflecting on key issues and concerns will assist you to identify areas that may require particular focus.

Before creating your vision, writing down your expectations is worthwhile, as it may give an idea of what you might include in the vision itself.

Here is a fill-in-the-gaps example to get you going:

- I expect ... and I will have work to do to adjust to our changing relationship.
- I expect I will live until I am ...
- I expect to maintain an excellent level of fitness and remain within a weight range of between ... kg and ... kg.
- I expect I will continue with work in some capacity for the next ... years.

- I expect my family who lives in ... will want to spend ... amount of time with me.

- I expect I will form a charity or serve on not-for-profit boards at some point in the next ... years.

- I expect I will write about ... in my memoir.

- I expect we will move to ... or into a motorhome to travel the country.

- I expect we will spend ... months at home and ... months abroad.

Your expectations can be used to develop some of your key indicators, milestones and goals to be mentioned in your vision.

Here's an example of how this might play out in your vision:

Expectation: *I expect to maintain an excellent level of fitness and remain within a weight range of 75kg to 80kg*

In your vision there might be a statement like: *My health is excellent physically, mentally and emotionally and on all other levels. I exercise four times a week in one form or another. I weigh 76.5 kg. I look and feel great. I am staying young. I am healthy and fit.*

Where possible, quantify your expectation in your vision (e.g. recording your weight between 69kg and 73kg). If not, qualify your vision (e.g. noting that you have a great lifestyle). The clearer the vision, the more likely it is that you can make your vision a reality.

As you create your vision, refer back to the work we covered in the early chapter on Self and the key aspects that were covered in the other six wealths beyond money.

In the end, when you read your vision, you want to say to yourself, 'That's the meaningful life I want, full of joy and fulfilment.'

Here is an example of a vision:

My Vision, December 20XX

I am so happy and grateful that I continue living a happy and meaningful life in the next stage of my life. It's fun.

I know that everything happens for a reason and ultimately for my highest good.

Through deep exploration, I have found peace of mind and a sense of contentedness and tranquillity. I am at peace and my life is wonderful.

I eat a well-balanced combination of foods that I tailor for my highest good. I do indulge every now and then and enjoy it when I do. I drink alcohol for enjoyment and appreciation. I am knowledgeable about the wines of the world and my wife and I visit a winery region once a year.

My health is excellent physically, mentally and emotionally, and on all other levels.

I exercise four times a week in one form or another. I weigh 76.5 kg. I look and feel great. I am staying young. I am healthy and fit.

I make time to meditate. I also make time to explore my creativity, including writing and composing music, which I love and have an extreme passion for.

My wife and I own a beautiful house that overlooks the city of Sydney. It is close to both water and nature parks. It is a peaceful haven for living, playing and working. I also have a getaway haven overlooking the beach on the Sunshine Coast, which is sensational. I share it with both my family and friends. I have a great lifestyle that suits both myself and my wife.

I own several properties that bring in passive cash flow on a weekly and monthly basis. They are solid investments.

My relationship with wife, my soulmate and my ultimate companion, continues to evolve. She is attractive and beautiful on all levels. Our care for each other and companionship continues to strengthen and evolve as we grow together. The relationship exists for our highest good. We have a beautiful family unit. We see our children and grandchildren on a regular basis and we love watching them develop into great human beings. Our input is valued by the children.

My friends are the best. They are very positive and loving and have come into my life for my highest good. They are also successful and wealthy in the fields in which they work. My friends openly give of themselves and enjoy life to the maximum, as I do. My friends are very special people.

The people I attract into my life are influential and are willing to help me achieve my goals. They radiate positive energy.

I am well respected by my peers and the people I work with. I work only 500 hours (3 months) a year, consulting with and presenting to various companies, including Google, Microsoft, Amazon, Crypto Inc and distributed ledger technologies. I am renowned for my ability to edutain and manage both people and projects. I am very well paid for everything that I do.

I donate considerable time and money to my chosen charities, including CanTeen and the Red Cross. My wife and I have set up a perpetual scholarship based on community service to our local school. Our legacy. I sit on the boards of two not-for-profit organisations focused on access to technology for disadvantaged kids and schools. The work is really rewarding.

I am so grateful and happy for I am financially free in every sense of the word. Money comes easily and frequently and in ever increasing amounts and from ever increasing sources. I own and I control everything.

My wealth continues to grow thanks to my leadership of and involvement in my consulting company GHX and my other ventures that span the globe.

My wealth allows me and my wife to live and lead the life we choose to (travelling overseas, attending events, assisting children, sponsoring scholarships, etc.). It is a freedom I greatly treasure and appreciate.

I continue to improve myself on all levels.

I am a contented soul in 20XX.

BEYOND THE MONEY

As you read the example, you can you see where it touches on each of the wealths and comes together into one cohesive vision.

Okay! So now it is your turn. Let's put it all together...

As you create your own vision it is worth considering the following questions:

- What are your needs?

- What are your hopes for the future?

- What is your definition of a productive, meaningful and joyful life moving forward?

STRATEGIES FOR A SMOOTH TRANSITION

Below are a series of strategies that will help you move forward.

- Over the final months of full-time work, gradually separate yourself from the job you've been performing. Make sure your work role is not your identity.

- Consider giving the ending of your full-time work life a title, e.g. The Graduation; Work's Final Chapter; The End of Busting Your Butt, etc.

- Keep open communication with significant people in your life regarding your feelings and plans. Talk to others you trust for support.

- Stay in touch with your thoughts. What you're focusing on regularly.

- Point your focus forward rather than backward.

- Give yourself time to experience the change process.

- List the positives and negatives, and the gains and losses, of your lifestyle change.

- Keep in touch with your work network and stay connected via your e-network (through LinkedIn, Facebook, Twitter, Instagram, etc.).

- List positive things that are happening in the moment. Visit your gratitude list every day.

- Celebrate small achievements.

- Give yourself a break and take your time (you've certainly got it moving forward).

- Arrange and develop temporary structures and routines throughout each week. Choose new life patterns if it is beneficial.

- Explore your local area and topics you are interested in. Do the research.

- Start to develop talents in new areas and in skills you take a keen interest in.

- Open yourself up for learning as you transition. See it as a learning experience.

- Read books/e-books that you have always wanted to read (make a list).

- Don't act for the sake of action. You'll get caught in busy-ness.

- Spend time alone – relax, think and take care of yourself. This is a time for you to be number one.

- Set short-term goals and timetables.

- Do small things well.

- Explore. Look around you to see what's out there for you to learn.

- Celebrate your progress.

- Slow down and enjoy the newness of the next stage of your life.

- Stay in touch and re-connect with old friends via phone, email or social media.

- Consciously notice the differences in your life. Choose the ones that work for you.

- Visualise success and what it means to you moving forward in the seven wealth areas.

- Set new priorities.

- Keep your eyes open for opportunities to contribute to your family, friends and community.

- Be aware of new stress factors for you and take action where appropriate.

- Translate your ideas into action plans.

- Be a good communicator and seek feedback from people you know and trust.

- Be and stay optimistic.

- Listen carefully to your self-talk. Change when required.

- Do the research on volunteering with an organisation that you have a connection with or have an interest in supporting.

CONVERSATIONS TO HAVE WITH YOURSELF AND OTHERS

At this point, we're going to consider the conversations that it may be useful to have – both with yourself and with others.

Conversations with yourself:

- How am I going to deal with the change on a personal level?

- What am I going to do with my time?

- Whom will I spend my time with?

Conversations with spouses, partners and significant others:

The following questions are worthwhile considering before misunderstandings, arguments and resentments occur. This is called an ecology check. It is priceless to go through this process and allow you and your loved ones to get clear on where each person is coming from.

- What is it I need to know about your routines?
- What are your expectations of me now that I'm around a lot more?
- What should I do and what shouldn't I do around the home?
- What is important to you about my new life stage?
- How can I be of assistance?

Conversations with family:

It's so important to have conversations with family members. They can often reveal truths about the situation that you would otherwise be unaware of.

- What are your expectations now that I'm moving into the next stage of my life?
- These are my expectations…

CELEBRATING THE MOVE

In Michael Watkins' book *The First 90 Days*, the author spends some time discussing celebrating moves in one's career before strategising for the first ninety days of the new role. In a sense, it is a time to say goodbye to the old role and welcome the new role. What better way than with a celebration?

When you move out of full-time work, it is worth celebrating. For some people, this could be as simple as a dinner out or a family gathering, while for others, it is about taking a real break and celebrating the old and the new by travelling nationally or overseas.

Whatever your decision, the main thing is to make the celebration mean something to you.

Here are some of the many ways my clients have celebrated:

- A dinner out with family and friends.
- A home-based celebration with family and friends, usually a barbecue or dinner.
- A bottle of good champagne.
- A trip overseas.
- A day trip to a place that means a lot to you.
- A Gold Class visit to the movies.
- A night at the pub with mates (just beware of the consequences!).
- Gone fishing; gone camping; gone boating.
- A weekend away.
- Watching a favourite movie.
- Heading to the beach.
- Going on a cruise (or two!).
- Re-reading favourite books.
- Sleeping in without stress or guilt.

2. Making it a Reality

*'People with goals succeed
because they know where they are going.'*

— EARL NIGHTINGALE

I have a good friend and mentor who has stuck to a certain ritual for many years. It is one that I admire. Now that he has turned sixty, he believes it is even more relevant as he no longer has to work; rather, he chooses to work, and he works according to his own timetable in the course of each year.

In the first week of each year, he and some close friends get together and discuss the coming year in detail, across different areas of their life (not dissimilar to the areas that are highlighted in this book). The first three to five days of each year are dedicated to planning what he and his partner want to create in the coming year.

He works from macro to micro, from what is happening in the year to what happens in the months and weeks, even to the point of designing his perfect day.

Although this takes time, all of his planning comes to fruition in the course of the year. He has been amazed and humbled by what he has achieved.

Each person has a different way of planning, creating and designing their lives. Below are the frameworks that you can use to design your years, months, weeks and days ahead.

When deciding what activities and interests to allocate time to, remember the seven wealth areas:

1. Self
2. Wellbeing
3. Location
4. Relationships
5. Lifestyle and Modified Work Life
6. Legacy
7. Spiritual Development

While doing this exercise, you may be tempted to put the same activity in each timeframe. In some cases this is warranted however, it should turn up in a different form in each case. The examples below provide a good illustration of how to hone down the activities. What you also want to do with your activities is align them with your wealth areas and your values.

EXAMPLES OF ACTIVITIES THAT HAPPEN ONCE A YEAR

SELF:

- Watch my favourite movie series (*Jason Bourne*/*Star Wars* [*maybe Episodes IV, V, and VI*]/*Lord of the Rings*/ *Lethal Weapon*)

- Study and complete an educational course

WELLBEING:

- Check weight in March of each year (remain in the weight range between 75kg and 80kg)

RELATIONSHIPS:

- Visit family overseas (school holidays)
- Anniversary dinner/celebration
- Christmas every second year with family
- Support grandkids at sport carnivals and school events (swimming/athletics/musical theatre/stage shows/graduations)

LIFESTYLE AND MODIFIED WORK LIFE:

- Melbourne Cup Racing Carnival – November
- Summer Nats Motor Show – January
- First day of the cricket test in my home city – December
- International or national winery tour
- Attend two cultural performances – stage shows, music, etc.
- Go weekend camping (not glamping)
- Attend two restaurant degustations each year
- Watch the Tour de France – July
- Watch the Australian Open Tennis – January
- Watch Masters Golf – April
- Either what or attend the AFL and NRL footy finals – last weekend in September

- Spend a week at the beach/lake/snow
- Local staycation

LEGACY:

- Attend at least two charity balls
- Attend various boards' annual general meetings

SPIRITUAL DEVELOPMENT:

- Spend two weeks relaxing with no mobile devices or screens (Spring or Autumn)

EXAMPLES OF ACTIVITIES THAT HAPPEN MONTHLY

- One Gold Class movie (self, lifestyle)
- A great dinner out (self, relationships)
- Visit family members and grandkids (relationships)
- Golf with social club (lifestyle)
- Charity board work (legacy)
- Have a full body massage (self, wellbeing)
- Read a new book (self)
- Men's Shed (wellbeing, lifestyle, self)
- Watch grandkids' sport/activities (relationships)
- Examples of activities that happen weekly
- Exercise four times a week (self, wellbeing)
- Game of golf (self, lifestyle)
- Modified work life – two days a week from home or on site (lifestyle and modified work life)

- Touch base via phone/Skype/Zoom/Facetime with family members and grandkids (relationships)

- Gardening and keeping the home looking good (self, lifestyle)

- Sleep in on Sunday (self, lifestyle)

EXAMPLE OF A PERFECT DAY

- Exercise (gym, PT, walk, swim, skip, run, Pilates, yoga) for one hour (self, wellbeing, live fitness value)

- Meditation for half an hour (self, wellbeing, spiritual development)

- Relaxing healthy breakfast with partner (self, lifestyle, wellbeing)

- Read (self, lifestyle)

- Share morning tea with partner (relationships)

- Do some work – paid or not-for-profit – for four hours (modified work life, legacy)

- Eat a healthy lunch with colleagues (relationships)

- Afternoon activity/adventure/project/ nine holes of golf for two hours (self, lifestyle)

- Watch the sunset with a beer/wine in my hand (self, wellbeing)

- Skype/Zoom/Facetime family (relationships)

- Dinner with friends and/or family (relationships)

- Watch a favourite TV series or movie (self, lifestyle)

- Bed

Take the tips and exercises we've been through in each wealth area and consider what different things you might want to devote yourself to in different time periods. As you go from macro to micro, from your plans for the year down to your plans for the perfect day, become more and more specific. The more detail you go into in this exercise, the more chance there is for your vision to come to life.

Exercise: Designing My Perfect Year

Time	Activities
January	E.g. Long weekend with family
February	
March	E.g. Yearly weigh-in (75-80kg) and health check
April	E.g. Watch US Masters
May	
June	
July	E.g. Visit family overseas
August	Winter charity ball
September	
October	
November	E.g. Attend Melbourne Cup
December	

Exercise: Designing My Perfect Month

Time	Activities
Week 1	E.g. Gold Class movie
Week 2:	E.g. Dinner out with partner
Week 3:	E.g. Board meeting, full body massage
Week 4:	E.g. Golf with social club

Exercise: Designing My Perfect Week

Time	Activities
Monday	E.g. Exercise
Tuesday	E.g. Work, PT
Wednesday	E.g. Game of golf
Thursday	E.g. Exercise, work
Friday	E.g. Touch base via phone/Skype/Zoom/Facetime with family members and grandkids
Saturday	E.g. Watch sport, dinner with friends
Sunday	E.g. Sleep in

Exercise: Designing My Perfect Day

Example:

Time	Activity
5.00	Sleep
6.00	Exercise (gym, PT, walk, swim, skip, run, Pilates, yoga)
7.00	Meditation
8.00	Relaxing healthy breakfast with partner
9.00	Read
10.00	Work – paid or not-for-profit
11.00	Work – paid or not-for-profit
12.00	Eat a healthy lunch with colleagues
1.00	Work – paid or not-for-profit
2.00	Work – paid or not-for-profit
3.00	Afternoon activity/adventure/project/9 holes of golf
4.00	Afternoon activity/adventure/project/9 holes of golf
5.00	Watch the sunset with a beer/wine in my hand with partner
6.00	Skype/Zoom/Facetime family
7.00	Dinner with friends and/or family
8.00	Dinner with friends and/or family
9.00	Watch a favourite TV series or movie
10.00	Watch a favourite TV series or movie
11.00	Read ready for bed
Midnight	Sleep

Your Turn:

Time	Activity
6.00	
7.00	
8.00	
9.00	
10.00	
11.00	
12.00	
1.00	
2.00	
3.00	
4.00	
5.00	
6.00	
7.00	
8.00	
9.00	
10.00	
11.00	

The frameworks that I have provided you with are not rocket science by any means, but they do give you a structure that you can make your own. If you have the discipline to create a ritual like my friend at the start of the chapter, then you will have a way to measure your progress, review what's important to you and what you really want to do in the coming years, and set down your purpose in the areas of your life that matter.

Now you have a plan, all that's left is to put it into action!

Conclusion

'You cannot become successful, you can only BE successful.
When doing becomes infused with the timeless quality of BEING,
that is success.'

—ECKHART TOLLE

Congratulations and thanks for reading this book. You've participated in preparation for your transition into the next stage of your life, ready to do it in a way that is grounded, connected and in alignment with who you are and what you want.

By doing the hard yards, you've begun your journey. You are now clear on the world of wealth at your fingertips beyond the money:

1. Your Self: You know what is important to you, have identified your values and have created supporting beliefs in alignment with your journey moving forward. You know the skills and knowledge that you want to learn, develop and share.

2. Your Wellbeing: You have developed frameworks and strategies for your personal wellbeing, covering food and nutrition, physical fitness and mental health. You can live the mantra 'Health is Wealth' on your own terms. You can turn to the 7 Ancient Principles of Wellbeing for a simple but effective framework.

3. Your Location: You have gained the tools to assess where you want to live in the next stage of your life and why, avoiding Rose-coloured Glasses Syndrome and recognising that where you are located can assist in enhancing many of the other wealths in your life in the next age.

4. Your Relationships: You are clear on your expectations of partners, family members, friends and social networks. You have learnt that this wealth is the real key to long-term enjoyment, meaningfulness and fulfilment in the next stage of your life.

5. Your Lifestyle and Modified Work Life: You now have clarity on the lifestyle you want to create in the next stage of your life, including meaningful recreational activities and a modified work life.

6. Your Legacy: You have thought about and put down ideas about the type of legacy that you wish to leave behind. You've considered how to make your own contribution in your own way, in a way that makes a difference and means something for you.

7. Your Spiritual Development: You have explored two concepts that many men have found useful in the next stage of their lives: the Law of Attraction and the simple practice of gratitude. Your gratitude list combined with your ability to shift perspective in the tough times will hold you in good stead moving forward.

You now have a practical blueprint for the next stage of your life. Well done!

Meaningful lives are first imagined, then designed and then lived via a well-developed action plan.

Throughout this book, you have gathered the tools to be able to make the shift from full-time work into the next stage of your life a successful one. From preparation to planning, and through exploring the seven wealth areas, you've come to an awareness of the issues involved in this massive transition – and the strategies you can employ to make it smooth sailing.

So, now it is time for the big A word: ACTION!

Good luck and I wish you all the best as you transition into the next stage of your life as a Next-Ager.

Epilogue

When I first started writing this book, my father Peter was alive and well and living in Sydney, albeit getting a bit old. We spent some time talking about this book and its content while I was writing it. Sadly, Dad recently passed away. I know that he wanted to leave some of his story to others, and I consider this book one of his legacies. A legacy of value to you and very much a legacy for his oldest son, me. Thanks Dad.

Appendix 1.
Busting the Myths and Facing the Realities Q&A

Answers to the Myth versus Reality quiz:

- Most successful men transitioning out of full-time work are totally satisfied doing nothing but travelling and relaxing in the next stage of their lives. **FALSE**

- Many men report that the single greatest problem in the early days of the next stage of their life is restructuring their daily lives. **TRUE**

- Preparing a résumé is nothing but a waste of time for successful men who don't plan to work for pay. **FALSE**

- Significant others have little trouble adjusting to their partner being at home most of the time. **FALSE**

- If someone has a consuming interest, like golf, they are always happy to spend all their spare time pursuing it – they do not need to plan other activities. **FALSE**

- Because many friendships revolve around the workplace, many successful men find that they have to consciously and actively work at expanding their social networks. **TRUE**

- At age sixty-five, you can expect to live at least another fifteen years. **TRUE**

- When modifying one's diet, it is easiest to eliminate all undesirable foods and add only desirable ones in one clean sweep. **FALSE**

- The majority of successful men report that they are very pleased with their new lives after leaving work. **TRUE**

Appendix 2.
Depression Symptoms
Checklist

The following symptoms may indicate that you are under too much stress and are suffering from depression – particularly if you have more than a few of them. A consultation with a physician may be desirable if symptoms are severe or persistent. There may be underlying physical factors that are causing or aggravating these symptoms.

Instructions:

Check off the symptoms that you are experiencing now or recall having experienced recently during stressful situations. Bear in mind that too much stress is usually indicated by a recurring pattern of symptoms rather than a single occurrence.

There is space at the end of each category for you to write in other symptoms (perhaps unique to you) that may indicate you are under too much stress.

If you find that you have several of the symptoms below then make contact with your doctor or health professional to discuss possible management moving forward. You can also use this list to keep an eye on your mates who may be joining you in the coming months and years as they transition into the next stage of their lives.

Physical Symptoms

Tired with low energy.

Sleeping too much.

Not sleeping enough and/or difficulty sleeping.

Overeating or loss of appetite.

Significant weight issues.

Constant physical fatigue.

Churning gut.

Stomach trouble, pain.

Sexual problems, impotence.

Overuse/abuse of alcohol or drugs.

Chronic physical ailments (indigestion, constipation, diarrhoea).

Backaches or headaches.

Mental Symptoms

Feeling overwhelmed, rushed and under constant pressure.

Feelings of sadness, unhappiness, isolation, loneliness.

Beating yourself up.

Catastrophic thinking, over-personalising situations.

Feeling inordinately vulnerable due to the criticism of others.

Feeling misunderstood.

Lacking confidence.

Difficulty asking for help.

Denial of problems.

Difficulty making decisions (both major and minor).

Feeling left out or rejected socially.

Frequent feelings of anger towards spouse/partner.

Worrying frequently (more than is normal for you).

Frequent feelings of sadness.

Inability to enjoy formerly pleasurable activities.

Feeling insecure about or undeserving of partner's affection.

Exaggerating your importance to self and to others.

Behavioural Symptoms

Deteriorating interpersonal relationships.

Not going out with, or withdrawing from close colleagues, friends, family.

Relying on alcohol and sedatives.

Frequent awkwardness, arguments with partner.

Problems with authority figures.

Avoiding tasks and responsibilities, particularly those formerly enjoyed.

Ongoing lateness.

Neglecting appearance, personal hygiene.

Frequently forgetting important information, commitments.

Going to extremes (excessive gambling, spending sprees, compulsive habits).

Uncompromised striving for perfection.

Should any of this be relevant to you, or to someone you know, there are several actions that you can take and there are many organisations that can assist you:

1. *Get in touch with your health professional.*

2. *Have a chat with a partner or mate whom you know and trust.*

3. *Get in touch with one of these organisations:*

    MensLine

    Lifeline

    Black Dog Institute

    Beyond Blue

    Men's Shed

    Movember Foundation

Books of Value

A Holistic Guide to a Happy Retirement by Paul McKeon

Ready to Retire? What Do You and Your Spouse Need to Know About the Reality of Retirement? by Lyndsay Green

It's Only Too Late If You Don't Start Now: How to Create Your Second Life at Any Age by Barbara Sher

Transitions: Making Sense of Life's Changes by William Bridges

I Could Do Anything If I Only Knew What It Was: How to Discover What You Really Want and How to Get It by Barbara Sher

The Happiness of Pursuit: Finding the Quest That Will Bring Purpose to Your Life by Chris Guillebeau

Managing Transitions: Making the Most of Change by William Bridges, PhD, with Susan Bridges

The Wall Street Journal: Complete Retirement Guidebook: How to Plan It, Live It and Enjoy It by Glenn Ruffenach & Kelly Greene

Minding the Body, Mending the Mind by Joan Borysenko

Boomers: Funding Your Future in an Age of Uncertainty by Mark Mills & Nancy Fernandez Mills

Don't Call Me Old, I'm Just Awakening: Spiritual Encouragement for Later Life by Marsha Sinetar

Do What You Are: Discover the Perfect Career for You Through the Secrets of Personality Type by Paul Tieger and Barbara Barron-Tieger

E-Squared: Nine-Do-It-Yourself Energy Experiments That Prove Your Thoughts Create Your Reality by Pam Grout

Links:

The Australian Government offers information about all facets of retirement:

https://www.australia.gov.au/information-and-services/jobs-and-workplace/retirement

https://www.humanservices.gov.au/individuals/subjects/age-pension-and-planning-your-retirement

MensLine:
https://mensline.org.au/tips-and-tools/adjusting-to-retirement

Sources of Information:

The Oxford English Dictionary
Definition of retirement: *The action or fact of leaving one's job and ceasing to work*

World Atlas: Timeline of Mass Extinction Events on Earth
https://www.worldatlas.com/articles/the-timeline-of-the-mass-extinction-events-on-earth.html

Forbes: Larry Jacobson via Next Avenue
https://www.forbes.com/sites/nextavenue/2016/06/21/the-big-problem-new-retirees-run-into/#6fbce65b75c9

Malcom Gladwell

David and Goliath: Underdogs, Misfits, and the Art of Battling Giants, 2013

TransAmerica Center for Retirement Studies

Current State of Retirement – A Compendium of Findings about American Retirees, 2016

Ameriprise Financial (Financial Arm)

Retirement Survey, 2016

Calouste Gulbenkian Foundation (UK Branch) & the Centre for Ageing Better

Evaluation of Pilot Projects – Supporting People through the Transition into Retirement

Actuaries Institute Australia, American Academy of Actuaries & Institute and Faculty of Actuaries.

Retirement Readiness: A Comparitive Analysis of Australia, the United Kingdom & the United States

William Bridges

Transitions: Making Sense of Life's Changes

John McClelland – Human Motivation Theory

https://www.mindtools.com/pages/article/human-motivation-theory.htm

Beyond Blue: Wellbeing

https://www.beyondblue.org.au/personal-best/pillar/wellbeing

Marilyn Glenville

Natural Alternatives to Dieting – Why diets don't work and what you can do that does

Law of Signatures

http://totalhealthmethod.com/the-secret-of-the-law-of-signatures

Basics to Islam: 6 Major Beliefs in Islam

https://sites.udel.edu/msadelaware/six-major-beliefs-in-islam

Judasim 101: 13 Principles of Faith

http://www.jewfaq.org/beliefs.htm

Buddhist Core Values: 3 Universal Truths and 4 Noble Truths

http://www.unhcr.org/50be10cb9.pdf

Hinduism for Dummies

https://www.dummies.com/religion/hinduism/core-beliefs-of-hindus

The Competencies of Learning

https://en.wikipedia.org/wiki/Four_stages_of_competence

Aerobic Exercise

https://www.dictionary.com/browse/aerobic-exercises

Stressors: Positive and Negative

https://www.google.com.au/search?q=positive+stress+vs+negative +stress

Grey Nomad Numbers Up

https://www.smh.com.au/national/nsw/grey-nomad- numbers-up-20170223

Harvard Study of Adult Development

https://news.harvard.edu/gazette/story/2017/04/over-nearly-80-years-harvard-study-has-been-showing-how-to-live-a-healthy-and-happy-life

Mind Matters – Mastering Human Potential- Manuals and Workbooks

The Infinite Power of Your Relationships

NeuroCoding Mastery

Performance Alchemy

Ancient Wisdom, Future Success

Relationship Types

https://www.google.com.au/search?q=types+of+relationships+with+people&rlz=1C5CHFA_enAU724AU727&oq=types+of+relationships+with+people

Alex Lickerman, MD, 'The Art of Microcompromise: How to survive the compromises that all relationships require'

https://www.psychologytoday.com/us/blog/happiness-in-world/201004/the-art-microcompromise

Reticular Activating System (RAS)

https://www.sciencedirect.com/topics/neuroscience/reticular-activating-system

Conceptual Knowledge and Learning

https://www.google.com.au/search?rlz=1C5CHFA_enAU724AU727&lei=IukW5TUN4OU8wXTvac4&q=conceptual%20learning%20examples

Conceptual Knowledge Examples

https://www.thebalancecareers.com/conceptual-skills-list-and-examples

Types of Philanthropy

http://www.philanthropy.ie/good-giving/becoming-a-donor/types-of-philanthropy

Pam Grout

E-Squared: Nine-Do-It-Yourself Energy Experiments That Prove Your Thoughts Create Your Reality

Michael Watkins

The First 90 Days – Critical Success Strategies for New Leaders at All Levels

Project 100

https://www.100people.org/statistics_detailed_statistics.php

https://www.youtube.com/watch?v=QFrqTFRy-LU

Beyond Blue – Depression

https://www.beyondblue.org.au/the-facts/depression/signs-and-symptoms

Black Dog Institute

https://www.blackdoginstitute.org.au/docs/default-source/factsheets/symptomsofdepression.pdf?sfvrsn=2

Health Direct

healthdirect.gov.au/symptoms-of-depression

Acknowledgements

To my beautiful wife Kerri who has supported me throughout the journey of writing this book. Thanks to her motivational skills, this book is a reality, not just a three quarters-finished project sitting on my hard drive.

To my two dads, Peter and JB. Their stories and lives were the inspiration for this book. In a sense, this book is their legacy, too.

To my mum Kay, who has always encouraged me to follow my passions and to look beyond the money when pursuing my ideas and dreams. Your love and support over the years has and continues to be invaluable.

To my brother Phil and sister Jacqui for their ongoing input and feedback into the development of the book. Thanks to Jacqui for artistic work within the book too.

To Sara Litchfield, my editor, who has been extremely patient with me as a first-time author and provided honest feedback, great advice and excellent guidance in the production of the final product that is *Beyond the Money*. I am so grateful for your support and advice. Priceless.

To Jacqui Pretty, Jake Creasey and the gang at Grammar Factory, who have enabled this work to be not only a book but a project that can make a real difference for a generation of men transitioning out of full-time work and into the next adventure and age of their lives.

To my long-time mentors at Mind Matters, Rex Urwin and Catherine Connelly, for their transformational work, which I have been a beneficiary of and which has allowed me to provide the support for clients in transition.

To Lee Hecht Harrison – especially Helen Burton and the team – who have given me great feedback and support along the journey. A special mention to my work colleague and mentor, the late Mike Tucker, who, over many rounds of golf, gave me a real insight into what was needed for successful men transitioning into the next stage of their lives.

To William Bridges & Associates, and in particular Susan Bridges who gave me permission to reproduce the Bridges Model of Transition.

To John Wade, who supported this idea from the start and has provided input at all stages of the process to making this book a hard copy reality.

To Andrew Griffiths, Glen Carlson, my accountability group, the KPI (Key Person of Influence) and dent team, who provided the initial impetus with a simple structure and the thirty-day 1,000-words-a-day challenge. Andrew's webinars and comments along the way have been gold. Thanks.

To the many clients I have conducted transition programs with over the past decade or so and who, when asked, agreed to share their stories not only with me but also with the wider public so that others could learn the lessons.

Finally, to you, the reader. Thanks for your investment of time. I hope this book leaves you feeling confident and inspired and with a renewed sense of purpose and passion as you move forward into the next stage of life's journey. Welcome to the Next Age!

About the Author

Steve is the founder of Next-Aging and the Beyond the Money Program. A Transition Specialist with over twenty-five years' experience in board level representation, executive coaching, training and development, educating, workshop facilitation and workforce transformation.

Steve has a passion for human development. He is an expert at creating the space for people to move forward and expand as human beings, both individually and in corporate situations.

Steve has served on the boards of CanTeen Australia (National Chair and President), the Australia Day Council (NSW) and the UAE Division of The Terry Fox Foundation, and completed a four-year term on the Australian Executive of the Japanese Government's Ship for World Youth Program (SWY).

Steve has conducted and presented hundreds of public presentations and international webinars on various topics, including: Active Retirement, Career Transition, Workplace Health and Safety, Managerial Resilience and Team Leadership.

Over and above Steve's executive coaching experience, he has been involved in project management, organisational change, consulting and workshop facilitation in the Middle East, the United Kingdom, and throughout Australia.

Steve's global career has been eclectic. He has been Managing Director of several companies, including: 90's fashion label MWI-MoodWear Ink, The Fortunate Group Pty Ltd, and

SMEE: Steve Mendl Enterprises and Entertainment. He has also held positions with Lee Hetcht Harrison, Events Management Australia, Emirates Institute of Technology, Sportscraft Australia and Emirates Media Inc.

With a BA in Business Administration, a Graduate Diploma in Education, and a Master Practitionership in Neuro Linguistic Programming (INLPTA), Steve has gone on to gain post-graduate certificates in small business management and personal skills development.

Steve has completed major Career Transition and Workforce Transformation Projects with clients from Rio Tinto, Microsoft, BUPA, Qantas, American Express, Woolworths, Hewlett Packard, Pepsico, Nokia, GrainCorp and the Department of Health.

9 780648 430766